THE
PATIENT
PATIENT

Humorous insight, practical advice
and my true life medical dramas

by Muriel Cunningham

authorHOUSE

1663 LIBERTY DRIVE, SUITE 200
BLOOMINGTON, INDIANA 47403
(800) 839-8640
www.authorhouse.com

14382

First published by AuthorHouse 05/25/04

ISBN: 1-4184-5754-X (e)
ISBN: 1-4184-3790-5 (sc)
ISBN: 1-4184-3788-3 (dj)

Library of Congress Control Number: 2003098639

Printed in the United States of America
Bloomington, Indiana

This book is printed on acid-free paper.

Table of Contents

Preface

Years and years ago, when I was in my early 20s, I read a book on longevity. It sparked a desire in me to read all sorts of health books and articles in newspapers and magazines. I even subscribed to a doctor's newsletter on health and healing. I became fascinated with the subject, and my interest is always perked when I notice something about health that could be of help to me, or to someone I know.

This knowledge is tapped occasionally when friends and family call me, asking for advice about their myriad ailments. It makes me feel so good that they would think to consult me, and many times I am, in fact, able to help them.

For instance, my daughter recently called asking for information on kidney stones that had her husband bent up like a pretzel. I quickly found the chapter in one of my books. The writer of this book told the story of a strong man who professed he could stand even the worst of pain and had even allowed his teeth to be drilled on by a dentist without novocaine. But when he was struck with kidney stones, the man said, "I cried." The solution, according to the book, was to drink gallons and gallons of water, juice, or whatever it took to flush those kidneys out.

At the time, my niece worked with a lithotripsy unit where they used a method of blasting the stones so that they could be passed. The technicians who worked with her reported, "If people would drink enough water, they would have no need for our services!"

Why is it that so many of us avoid the healthiest thing we can do for ourselves: simply drinking water? Not coffee, decaf, Coke or Gin Fizzes—just plain water. And why is it that those other drinks taste so good?

A while back, my daughter wanted to know about my experiences after hemorrhoid surgery. Her jaw dropped when I told her that I had been allowed to remain in the hospital for a whole week afterward. After describing how she'd been told to sit in a chair after surgery, and had been sent home that same day, I recoiled inside, thinking, Oh, you poor, poor thing.

It is interesting to note that almost one sixth of the U.S. work force is employed by the health-care industry. When I'm asked to share some of my self-styled *wisdom* with the young ones, I hope more than anything to help them avoid becoming a *patient* patient. I hope the same for the readers of this book.

*

Thoughts of people with health problems, unusual happenings, and interesting experiences—some good, some bad, and many times quite humorous—have been mulling around in my mind for more than a year. It has amazed me how these thoughts have flowed with ease from my mind to paper while writing this book. It has been most enjoyable to me for I understand this book's purpose and worth to all who will read and enjoy it.

The book I originally read on longevity stressed eating blackstrap molasses, brewer's yeast, buttermilk, yogurt, and liver. After I tasted all that stuff, I didn't care how long I lived! In fact, my daughter has still never forgiven me for insisting that she taste just a bite size morsel of liver! I do not believe or practice everything I read, and certainly that particular author lost me when he suggested that everyone wolf down steaks like dogs do. I suspect that more folks choke on the steak than benefit by it!

I'd like to get things all figured out before I'm 90, and I've yet to make the decision whether I should be cremated or buried, but until then,

The sun is shining, and skies are blue,
The birds are singing, and I have writing to do.

When I need a break from writing, I call a friend, plan something fun, or invite friends to lunch in my home. I enjoy people.

Just the other day, I called an old friend:

Since the invention of the telephone, we have not come up with a better way to answer the phone than *hello*. This time the phone was answered by Marguerite in her usual inquisitive and cheerful voice, "Helloo?"

"Hi, it's Muriel. I'm calling to invite you and the girls to lunch some day next week."

"Wonderful!" she responded. "I'll do the calling. My sister and I always visit Mama in the nursing home on Wednesdays and Fridays, and I have a dentist appointment on Monday. I'll have to check to see when the others are available." She seemed eager to chat. "So, what have you been doing lately, Muriel?"

"Marg, I've been having the time of my life," I declared. "I'm writing a book!"

"So, you finally learned to use your new computer! So dear, what is the title of your book?" she asked.

"How to Get Out of the Hospital Alive," I proudly answered.

Silence. I never in my life expected her to say what she said, "You're kidding. I just happen to be holding that very book in my hands right now! Same title exactly. The book is written by a Doctor Sheldon Blau."

"Now you must be kidding me," I replied in complete surprise. "You mean my book has already been written?"

I hung up thinking I had a problem to solve, but I was still determined to continue writing my own book. It was quite a shock, to be honest.

Well, I thought, I'll just have to come up with a different title! As I reread many of my own stories, the words "patient patient" seemed to leap right off the page. You will find that when you become a patient, you must be patient. I bought a copy of Dr. Blau's book. I enjoyed reading it, and I would highly recommend it. I particularly loved his sense of humor. Although Dr. Blau and I are writing about the same subject, his advice is coming from a professional point of view, and mine is coming from the other end of the needle!

*

All of the stories in this book are real; some are humorous, and some describe extremely frustrating and humbling situations. Most of these situations happened back in the days when you were actually admitted to a hospital. Today, so many surgeries and treatments are done on an outpatient basis. To me, it seems heartless to turn a patient out three hours after a hernia surgery. However, considering the infections and mistakes one can be exposed to during a hospital stay, it may be the safer way to go!

The names of most of the patients in my stories have been omitted, because names in most situations are inconsequential to the message.

I am thankful for all of the experiences I have lived through—even the stupid and painful ones have helped me to become a more compassionate person. I think you'll find that I became a *patient* patient as a result of trying some of my own remedies. So proceed with some common sense, please. The school of hard knocks doesn't teach much about the medical field. Therefore, with my limited knowledge, I practiced on myself. If you want advice or treatment from a professional, you must pay.

But I say this with tongue in cheek, mine is free!

Acknowledgment

To My Daughter, Ruth

1

Playing Doctor: My Own Remedies

Healing for the Gallbladder

An "I Gave Blood Today" sticker was proudly pasted on my coat by the nurse at the Bloodmobile. It made me particularly happy to be able to give blood twice in one year. However, I soon became unusually tired—extremely so.

After about a week of feeling completely exhausted, I finally dragged myself to the doctor's office, one whom I'd never seen before, and nearly fell asleep in the waiting room. Later, in the examination room, the doctor found me lying on the patient's table, almost asleep.

When he entered the room, he asked in his professional office demeanor, "How are you?"

I thought he intended his question as a greeting, so I replied, "Just fine, doctor, how are you?" If in my greeting, there was a hint of familiarity, it was quickly squelched by his question.

"Then why are you here?" he asked. He was obviously displeased with the way I had answered him. I looked perfectly healthy to him.

My only complaint didn't seem to impress him either. "I'm very, very tired," I said. I neglected to mention the fact that my fatigue had begun after giving blood. Perhaps it would have helped him to make a proper diagnosis.

"We'll run some lab work," he replied brusquely. It was a long sentence for this doctor.

When the lab work was complete, he returned to use his stethoscope on me here and there, he took my blood pressure, and then he dismissed me. He didn't say another word.

Back in the reception area, I was writing a check for the office visit and I began to feel very odd. "I feel like I'm going to faint," I mumbled.

Three nurses quickly appeared and led me into an examination room. They sat me in a chair, pushed my head down between my knees, and, I think, administered some smelling salts. A few moments later, I felt okay again. Then, from down the hall, someone from the lab called, "Don't let her leave! She has albumen in the urine."

There was no further consultation with the doctor. The head nurse took over and made arrangements to hospitalize me for more testing. I was given instructions to go home and wait for a call informing me when I would be admitted to the hospital. No one, including myself, considered that I might pass out while driving home. In any case, I arrived safely, crawled into bed for another nap, and wondered what would happen next.

Late that afternoon, I was beginning to feel really sick; *punk* would be a better word to describe it. I was running a fever of about 100 degrees. The doctor had given me a prescription for an antibiotic called Tetracycline, which I was told to take with Tylenol. Shortly after taking the two drugs, I began to hallucinate at night. I had a suspicion, from all of my reading, that this could be a side effect of a liver disorder.

I continued to wait patiently at home to be admitted into this apparently overcrowded hospital. We lived nearby the hospital, and with every passing day the sound of ambulances going past made me think, there goes my bed. It became clear to me that the month of

March was very busy in the hospital business. The extreme fatigue lingered, and I became more and more passive. Just let me sleep, was my only thought.

Every few days or so, the doctor would ask me to come to his office so that he could check my blood count, temperature, and blood pressure. Every time, he would inform me that my blood count was "far from normal," whatever that was supposed to mean.

As if all that wasn't enough, one of my molars began to ache. Because of my persistent fever, I dressed warmly as I prepared to go to the dentist. I knew his air-conditioned office would give me the chills. I could tell he felt sorry for me as he drilled away. The process seemed never-ending: Once every week I would get dressed, endure the drilling necessary to prepare for a root canal, then return home to wait patiently for the doctor's call to notify me about my hospital admittance. I never felt sorry for myself; I was simply amazed by how long I was being made to wait.

Every morning, I awoke drenched in sweat, but feeling reasonably well. I would change my wet nightclothes and sheets, put dry clothes on, and then go back to bed and wait another day while the ambulances wailed by. A few good friends brought me nourishing food and provided me with some company.

After a whole month of waiting, my fever shot way up. I didn't need a thermometer to tell me so. When my daughter came to visit, she prepared some hot tea and toast for me. Then, a friend of mine dropped off a book entitled, *How to Get Well*, by Dr. Paavo Ariola. The first thing I read was the chapter on "Liver Trouble." Without a firm diagnosis from my doctor, my suspicion that my problem had something to do with my liver continued. Perhaps I had gallstones, I thought. I read all about the doctor's remedy for liver cleansing and decided I had nothing to lose. I was ready to try anything. The directions in the book called for combining a quarter cup of raw olive oil with apple juice, and drinking it. My next-door-neighbor provided me with some of the required raw olive oil from the local health food store. I had never seen raw olive oil before—it had green streaks floating around in it.

My neighbor shuddered while she watched me swallow the concoction, which made me sweat and shiver while I drank it. The taste wasn't so bad, but all that oil was hard to keep down. I hiccupped an hour later and had to swallow hard to keep from bringing it up again.

But what tremendous results! For the first time in ages, I enjoyed an entire night's sleep! The next morning, my fever was gone! My bedclothes were unbelievably dry.

The book recommended that the process be continued for two nights and then the amount should be doubled on the third night. Because it had worked so well the first night, you better believe I forced that olive oil right down, just as directed. Even today, I feel like gagging when I remember swallowing all that oil. It was no easy task. I learned to wipe my lips and tongue quickly and drink another glass of cold apple juice to wash it down.

The other remedy found in "The Gallbladder Problems" section of Dr. Ariola's book called for one-half to three-fourths of a *pint* of oil at a time. Thank goodness it worked for me so quickly, or I don't think I would have been able to handle that much oil. Just writing about it has my saliva glands working overtime.

After the third treatment, the instructions from the book called for two enemas in the morning. To my utter surprise, I saw that I had passed gallstones—and a lot of them! I didn't know exactly what they were supposed to look like, but the lab technician at the hospital told me later that gallstones are green and look something like slightly smashed peas. I suppose I could have saved a few to show the doctor, but I didn't want to fish them out of the water!

The very next morning, after I'd completed the regimen, the phone rang. The nurse from the doctor's office informed me that I was finally going to be admitted to the hospital. I did not realize it at the time, but I had already partially cured myself with the help of Dr. Ariola. I agreed to be admitted.

After a month of fever, I still felt listless, tired, and weak. I was delighted to find that my hospital room on the ninth floor had a panoramic view of the city, and I was able to enjoy the beautiful sunrise from the window each morning of my stay. What a treat to watch the sun in all its splendor as it seemed to explode with all shades of red and yellow, breaking through a few drifting clouds, revealing a slice of Maxfield Parish sky.

Early on the first morning, my doctor appeared for his daily visit. He did not inform me about what kinds of tests were to be ordered that day, nor did he give me a clue as to what he was thinking could possibly be my problem. He listened in disbelief as I told him about the olive oil treatment, and he was very skeptical that I could have passed gallstones on my own.

Soon, the battery of tests began. One very nice volunteer pushed my wheelchair to the basement laboratory. The first test was a sonogram of my gallbladder area. Maybe any cholesterol stones I had didn't show up, or maybe I still had a lot of olive oil in my system, but either way, nothing unusual appeared on the monitor.

When the test was finished, I was pushed into the hallway where many other patients were lined up, and 1 was left to sit in that uncomfortable wheelchair to wait for another test, or to be taken back to my room. I was so tired. I tried to get comfortable by sliding way down in the chair, by leaning my head back, by propping my head on my arm, by leaning against the wall, and by letting my chin rest on my chest. I'd seen people sleep in wheelchairs before, but personally, I couldn't figure out how to do it.

I waited in the hall for an hour and a half, during which all of the nice volunteers disappeared for a coffee break. None of the staff even acknowledged me, or any of my wheelchair-bound compatriots. Technicians quickly scurried along, their eyes either glued to the floor or to their clipboards, avoiding eye contact with any of us lonely patients. If body language means anything, I was probably the worst one. In my mind, we were all viewed as pieces of worn-out furniture. I was the love seat; the big man ahead of me was the sofa; the lady with the IV stand was the lamp. I tried to find a euphemism for the attractive lady with the expensive looking robe, but before I could she was taken for her tests.

I must admit that when the technicians eventually performed my next tests, they behaved in a very professional manner. Finally, a volunteer wheeled me back to my room. I gratefully climbed into my bed and fell asleep, until a white-coated man came to draw yet more blood.

On the second day, I once again found myself abandoned in the hallway outside the lab. I muttered to myself, "No way, I'm not going to wait two hours for a volunteer this time." I wheeled myself onto the elevator, pressed the button for the ninth floor, rolled myself down the hall and into my room, and felt very clever as I snuck into my bed. I was asleep before they found me.

I was given a large glass of awful chalky stuff to drink, which was meant to aid in other tests, but I was not given much in the way of nourishing food. Some days, I was given nothing to eat at all. In the afternoon, I slept. Friends and family who had come to visit me informed me afterwards that they had found me fast asleep (probably with my mouth wide open).

On the third day, a lab technician caught me trying to make my escape. I almost made it to the elevator when I heard, "Oh, no you don't!" I felt someone grab my wheelchair. I needed a better plan, and quick. Sitting in that stupid wheelchair was the pits.

On the fourth day, after yet another test, I became determined. There would be no more waiting around in the hall for me! While I was still on the examining table after the test, I declared to the technician, "If you don't take me to my room right now, I'm going to sing!" I even surprised myself. Where do all my good ideas come from? Apparently, no one took me seriously, so I warned them again. "I have a terrible voice, and I sing off-key." Again, I was ignored. So

I took a deep breath and began belting out an old gospel tune at the top of my lungs, clapping loudly as I sang:

"I've got a mansion, just over the hilltop,
In that bright land where we'll never grow old..."

I'm sure everyone in the whole department heard me. Needless to say, my singing was unappreciated. A few technicians stuck their heads out of their rooms to see who was raising such a ruckus. Three nurses came running to take me to the elevator. A friend told me later that I was lucky I wasn't taken up to Ward D. On the fifth day, all I had to do was threaten to sing. My singing may have been worse than what I said it was, but it worked. There was no more waiting in the hall for me.

After nine days, each and every exhausting test had been completed. But my doctor was still puzzled as to why my blood count was abnormal. He consulted with a specialist who thankfully did not recommend a liver biopsy. I learned later how painful that procedure can be.

On the tenth day, the doctor came into my room to discharge me. Perhaps my blood count had improved. I don't know because he never told me. I left the hospital in about the same shape I'd been when I'd entered, just now full of needle pricks.

Hope was waning. I lazed aimlessly around the house for another week, and I still didn't understand why that terrible tiredness continued, even after the fever had gone away. After a week at home, I finally came to my senses. I decided that if I'd had a moderate measure of success with the olive oil treatment once, I would try it again.

I psyched myself up as I measured the olive oil and apple juice and poured the oil into a paper cup so I could throw it away immediately. I had to keep telling myself, "You can do it, you can do it, you can do it." However, my overworked saliva glands retorted, "You can't do it, you can't do it, you can't do it." I did do it! It took a will of steel to swallow and keep down twice the amount of oil on the third day.

Sure enough, miracles being miracles, the next morning I passed 16 more green cholesterol stones. I know, I counted! I was absolutely elated. After that, I slowly regained my strength, and a few weeks later, I was back to normal.

The doctor, the hospital stay, and all those tests didn't restore my health. I owed my thanks to the friend who loaned me Dr. Ariola's book, which dared me to try what the doctors thought was impossible.

Oh, My Toe!

One day while sunbathing nearly nude in my secluded backyard, I heard a car pulling into the driveway. I made a mad dash for the door, and stubbed my toe on the concrete steps. I knew instantly that it was broken by the loud cracking sound it made. It hurt like the dickens as I hobbled into the house to get dressed. I almost cried.

Over the next two weeks, the toe seemed to be healing on its own. But there were times when, if I moved my foot a certain way, the bone felt like it was literally splitting apart, and an inexplicable warm feeling would wash over me. Watching me limp around and grimace, the whole family finally chimed in: "Mother, you should go to the doctor!"

No one likes to go and sit in a doctor's office unless it's absolutely necessary. And I really didn't think this toe of mine required a doctor. My advice now is: Don't ever tell anyone to go to the doctor with a broken toe. My foot was X-rayed and the diagnosis was pronounced. I had a broken toe.

I already knew that. Now I wanted the doctor to tell me what to do about it. No one else was present in the office when the doctor asked, "Just how and when did you break that toe? It isn't a bad break, but the location of the fracture is way back in your foot." He proceeded to point out on the X-ray where the bone was broken.

Too embarrassed to divulge the entire story, I simply said, "I broke it two weeks ago when I crashed into some concrete steps."

"I have a suggestion for you," the doctor continued. "Wear shoes!"

He offered to put my foot into a cast, but said he didn't think it was absolutely necessary. I returned for a second and third visit and he ultimately said, "If you would like me to, I could put a pin in it."

Needless to say, the idea of a pin in my foot made me cringe, and seriously, I still did not think it was necessary. I carefully considered the situation. My foot was healing, but my movement had to be restricted in order for my toe to fully heal. I didn't necessarily have to wear a cast, but perhaps a more supportive shoe would help. The summer sandals I wore regularly allowed my foot to move around too much. I borrowed a pair of my daughter's big, bulky, marching-band bucks and I wore them for four weeks. They certainly weren't much of a fashion statement, but my toe healed up just fine and hasn't bothered me since, not even in stormy weather.

When I returned to the doctor's office, just to share with him my own creative way of handling a broken toe, he complimented me by saying, "You certainly missed your calling."

Really! Doctors won't do anything for a broken toe. One orthopedic doctor told me that his wife had been begging him to do something for her aching toes, and he said he wouldn't help her. I say, save your money and time by simply wearing heavy shoes to heal that broken toe.

My daughter learned the hard way how important it is to wear the right-sized shoes. During her first pregnancy, she chose to wear soft, high-top sneakers that were comfortable, yet supportive. Then her feet grew a size and a half without her realizing it. After the baby was born, and she returned to work, she went back to wearing her expensive stylish shoes and complained that her big toes were going numb. Finally, she went to see a podiatrist who said he was willing to lance her toes right there in his office. He went so far as to suggest that she could have all of the bones in her feet broken and reset.

Shocked and horrified, she asked, "Is that all I can do?"
His reply: "Well, you could buy bigger shoes."

A Wart on the Nose

Yes, that's right where it was. How in the world would I get rid of it? I remembered reading an article about applying vitamin E to a wart to make it dry up. I faithfully broke open a capsule and rubbed a little bit of it on my nose every day. To my horror, however, the wart began to grow. I felt like the wicked witch who had forgotten where she'd parked her broom. Why did this big ugly thing have to be plastered right in the middle of my face? There was no way to hide it!

At that time, I didn't realize how vain I'd become. I refused to look in the mirror and I avoided going out in public. I felt like people could see the thing a mile away, so I wanted to stay a mile away. I began to turn down invitations for things I really liked to do. Certainly, I thought, people would look at my wart and say to themselves, "Witch!" I wanted this ugly thing off my nose, and I wanted it off instantly.

So, I had to make a decision. Should I continue with the vitamin E, or should I have it removed surgically, as my neighbor had? In fact, my neighbor divulged, it had taken two surgeries to remove his! What about another option? I had a friend, who was a doctor, tell me about a method he'd used on the plantar wart on the bottom of his foot. He covered it with duct tape and, believe it or not, it had worked for him. Duct tape on my nose? No way! I made up my mind to give the vitamin E a bit more time.

Sometimes my home remedies work, and sometimes they don't, but I was determined. I started giving myself two or three treatments of the vitamin E daily, but to no avail. That wart just kept on growing and growing, just like the Energizer Bunny that keeps on going and going.

I was just about ready to give up when I read an article that stated that the wart must be covered. So I made a tiny bandage with masking tape and tissue soaked in vitamin E oil. I found that the masking tape did not pull on my sensitive facial tissue when I removed it. My daughter watched all this with skepticism. She insisted that what I really needed was surgery.

When she came home from college at the end of the week, she helped me peel off the bandage. She looked shocked. After all, how could she have been wrong? The hideous growth was gone! I could hardly believe it myself—the wart just peeled right off along with the tape, leaving only a tiny mark to remind me that sometimes my home remedies really do work.

The Frozen Shoulder

(I realize that by now, someone reading this book may have gotten the idea that I have done nothing in my lifetime but obsess over health issues. I promise, that is not the case. It wasn't until I was 47 years old and injured my back that I just seemed to fall apart at the seams.)

Out of all of the physical ailments I have experienced, my frozen shoulder was one of the most aggravating. I didn't understand why I couldn't move my arm or my shoulder, why both were so extremely painful, and what I had done to cause the problem. Looking back on it now, I see just how it happened. I also have, after months and months of doctors and treatments, a thorough knowledge of what a frozen shoulder is, and I know exactly what a doctor can or cannot do for it. But, most importantly, I learned what I could do for myself.

Without realizing it at the time, I had overexerted myself one day scrubbing my basement floor after a gallon of strong liquid cleanser had spilled. I do practically everything with my right hand, but when my right arm grew tired, I used my left arm and hand to finish the job. After all of those strenuous circular motions, my left arm was so sore that simply raising my arm to comb my hair was excruciatingly painful.

Shortly after I strained my arm just as we were to leave for Florida. My sore arm did not alter our plans to leave, however. Packing was difficult, and my husband had to help by closing the luggage and loading everything into the car. I reasoned that if I could just get into that cure-all Florida sunshine, my arm would get better. Riding in the car wasn't bad at all; my arm felt pretty good, probably because I wasn't using it.

I convinced myself that if I stopped raising my arm, it wouldn't hurt. Maybe it would heal faster if it were kept in a stationary position. So, I bought a sling. That was a big mistake! Two days later, any movement at all was impossible. Using that sling was not one of my brightest ideas.

The first doctor I consulted said, "Let me see how far you can move your arm." I responded by showing him. Then he asked, "Is that all you've got? Let's take some X-rays, then we'll rule out anything else. In my opinion, you have what we call a frozen shoulder."

I had never heard of a frozen shoulder. The doctor gave me a shot of cortisone, and it gave me some slight improvement. I returned to his office and waited patiently, only to be told that the X-rays supported his diagnosis. I felt like crying. My poor shoulder was frozen. I begged him to give me another shot of cortisone. In fact, I insisted that he *do* something for me, and that frustrated him. He knew very well that there wasn't anything he could *do* to help me, and at the same time, he wasn't very accomplished in getting that fact through to me. I'm sure that he had dealt with cases like this before, but he did not take the time to explain exactly what a frozen shoulder was. How I wished he would have at least tried. All the while, I was thinking, if that shot helped a little, another shot should help a little more. He looked at me like I was wasting his time and I guess, in retrospect, I was. All I knew was that my poor shoulder hurt so badly and I needed help. All he could tell me was that another shot of cortisone wouldn't do any good and that I would need therapy at some kind of sports center. Eventually, I reluctantly took his advice.

What frustrated me is that he never explained that it was absolutely necessary to stretch those tendons that had grown into the rotator cuff of the shoulder. Instead, I treated my symptoms the best way I knew how. I found if I walked around with an ice pack on the shoulder, the pain was bearable. I learned later that deep heat is much more beneficial than ice.

My daughter, her husband, and my eight-month-old grandson were visiting me at the time, and I offered to care for the baby while they enjoyed a meal out, a *date*, so to speak. When I finished feeding the baby, I took the dish to the kitchen and returned to see him just about hanging by his nose in the high chair. Frightened, I found I didn't have the strength to push him back into the chair, release the tray, or pull him out of the chair. Luckily, a neighbor came to our rescue. Naturally, the baby was now enjoying the chair very much and refused to get out. He even wanted more to eat! By that time, I was so frustrated that I didn't care what the baby wanted. Dinner was over!

The chiropractic treatments I sought next were brutal. The doctor stood behind me while I was seated, put both hands on my bent elbow, and pushed upward with a tremendous jerk that hurt like crazy. He also used ultrasound on the bursa on my upper arm and instructed me to do shoulder rolls when I got up in the morning. I was dumb enough to return for five more jerks from that jerk that didn't seem to help at all.

Then I tried a sports therapy center where hot packs and more ultrasound were administered. Maybe I didn't give it enough time, but the treatments just didn't seem to be working. I still felt lousy and I quickly became discouraged with this approach.

I tried an orthopedic surgeon who heartily recommended breaking the joint loose while under an anesthetic. The surgery was scheduled, but I chickened out and canceled. We had discussed what type of drug he would give me for pain after the surgery. I informed him that Codeine did not agree with me—it kept me awake. Then he gave me a prescription for Percodan. When I asked the druggist, he told me that

Percodan contains Codeine. That was one of the reasons why I decided not to have the surgery. The other reason was that it sounded so brutal the way the doctor had described it, and he said that sometimes the painful procedure had to be done twice. No, thank you! This was one of my wiser decisions.

When I returned to Ohio in the Spring, I decided to try my family doctor. He ordered X-rays so that he could be certain the cause wasn't something in my neck, and then he sent me to the hospital for therapy. At this point, I was willing to try anything. I just couldn't believe how long this pain had continued. Some things just get better by themselves, but it had been four months with this crazy thing, and I was still suffering extreme pain.

In the hospital therapy room a heavy thing called a hydroculator pad was plunked on my shoulder. And I do mean plunked. I don't know what material was in that hydroculator pad that made it so heavy (I later learned it was full of Mississippi mud!), but it was lifted out of boiling water and then wrapped in a towel—wet heat. Ultrasound was then applied on the muscle along my back under my left arm, which was stretched to a painful position. The therapist took hold of my hand and tried to move my arm by force. That resulted in a small measure of success. I endured this torture every day for two weeks. Finally, I thought, there must be a different and better way.

The good news is, there was! And, yes, it was my own idea that worked.

My eventual understanding of a frozen shoulder was gleaned from several doctors and therapists who were willing to take the time to explain what caused the pain. Evidently, the tendons had grown down into the ball and socket joint of my shoulder, where the arm is attached. They needed a lot of stretching to get back to normal, so I decided to develop my own exercise regime.

Lying flat on my back on the floor, I used the weight of a salad dressing bottle to do simple weight-lifting exercises. Grasping the neck of the bottle in my left hand, I would raise my arm straight up as far as it would go, and then with the other hand, I would gently nudge it up a little farther every day. I didn't try to move it out away from my body—that hurt too much—and besides, my arm simply would not move in that direction. It took about three months of my own daily stretching treatments, but I finally attained a full 180-degree range of motion. The deep moist heat of a thermophore heating pad allowed me to sleep free from the awful pain at night.

I'm so grateful that God gave me two arms, and I am most thankful now that I have the use of both of them. If you become aware that you have overused or abused your shoulder muscles, you can avoid suffering the pain of a frozen shoulder by raising your arms often, like doing the *wave* at the ballpark. It is important to keep the joint loose. Keep on using it—just don't abuse it! Whatever you do, don't put your arm in a sling. How I wish that someone had given me that advice when I needed it.

The Throbbing Throat

One summer, my husband and I were required to attend a funeral in Florida. I chose to wear the only black dress I owned. Since the dress was sleeveless, I also wore a lacy shawl to cover my shoulders, knowing the air-conditioning in the church would be cold and drafty, and knowing that funeral services can be lengthy. That evening, we dined outdoors and I became chilled again. As a result, I ended up with a sore throat.

Traveling back to Ohio the next day, we stopped at a small gas station that, like many others these days, was very accommodating. They sold everything from ice cream, shaving cream, and sunglasses, to aspirin, coffee, and cigarettes. It was raining, so in order to stretch my legs, I browsed around the store while my husband pumped the gas.

When he came inside to pay, I said, "I'd like to buy something for my sore throat. I don't want it to get any worse."

Both of us project our voices when we talk to each other because I can't hear, and because he is practically deaf. So naturally, everyone in this little store heard me when I mentioned my sore throat.

A kind man approached us, took a bottle of hydrogen peroxide off the shelf and advised, "Try gargling with this. You'll be better in the morning." He didn't sound like a doctor. Doctors don't usually say, "You'll be better."

I read the bottle's label with interest. It did indeed state that it could be used as a gargle or rinse. I had previously tried gargling with a variety of unusual substances, but never hydrogen peroxide, and I didn't like it. It made my mouth feel fizzy, and I thought, why did I listen to that man and gargle with this stuff that was killing my taste buds?

Much to my surprise though, it worked! Two days of gargling and I was almost well. My daughter tried it and it worked for her, too.

A member of our family who had been at the funeral had been stricken with strep throat and with all the hugging and kissing going on, I thought I had better get checked by my family doctor when I got home. Maybe my sore throat was something more serious despite the effectiveness of the hydrogen peroxide. He noticed on my chart that I hadn't seen him in three years. Maybe that was the real reason I went. I like to keep in contact with the family doctor, especially since I have such a wise one.

"I could give you an antibiotic, but you probably won't take it," he offered.

"Probably not," I agreed. "It won't do any good, will it?"

"No," he replied. "But I'll give you a prescription for one, just in case."

"Please give me one of the old ones," I asked. "Let someone else pay for the research on these new antibiotics."

I still have that bottle of pills waiting for me to get sick. I really like my doctor, but I can put up with the hydrogen peroxide.

A Tension Headache

I never thought there was anything unusual about headaches until I was in my thirties and I was hit with a nagging one that would not go away. At this time, I didn't know the difference between a surgeon and a medical doctor. We were so healthy, we did not have an established M.D., and so I returned to the doctor who had removed my daughter's tonsils to seek a cure for my headache. I simply thought that doctors were doctors. Perhaps an M.D. would have chosen to investigate a little by asking questions like, what I had been eating, or what had I been doing to cause the headache? For example, I've learned recently that artificial sweeteners used in soft drinks can cause headaches when too much is consumed.

Being a surgeon, this doctor looked at me, knowing that headaches were not his specialty, and suggested that I take my complaint to the Cleveland Clinic. The Cleveland Clinic, I thought. I must have something radically wrong with me.

At the clinic, all sorts of tests were performed. My head was not X-rayed, even though that's where the pain was, but my chest was. I had an ear infection and my ears were examined, but nothing was recommended. My blood pressure was taken, and a urinalysis was done, as well as routine blood work.

A gynecologist did part of the examination. Yes, I was given a gynecological exam for a headache. The nurse took me into a small room and ordered me to take off all my clothes, except my shoes. I was to lie down on the examination table with my feet up in the stirrups. I waited 45 insufferable minutes in that humbling position. Then, a young French doctor entered. Why he felt he had to make it known to me that he was French, and not married, I don't know. He behaved very professionally while he gave me a thorough pelvic exam. But as I look back on it now, that unnecessary check-up by that strange doctor was one of my life's most mortifying experiences.

Sitting around in the clinic's waiting rooms all day was quite tiring and dull. At 3:45 p.m., I was waiting to have my ear examined again. I really wanted to start for home before rush hour traffic and I was very irritated to see through the doorway the feet of the doctor propped on his desk with smoke wafting about. He was having his cigarette break as I sat there and waited. Fifteen minutes later, he examined my ear and told me I had an ear infection (as if I didn't know), and by this time I also had a slight fever in addition to my splitting headache.

After three trips to Cleveland as an outpatient, all of my information was compiled so that it could be evaluated by the doctor in charge of my case, which was now known as # 36241. I had never been treated in such an impersonal way. This particular doctor found nothing interesting or unusual in my reports, and since it was almost 5:00 p.m., he apparently wanted to get me out of there in a hurry. He told me that there was absolutely nothing wrong with me. Well, I knew that. I just had a headache and an ear infection.

Leaving the clinic with a little bottle of pills, my head was pounding, especially after all the waiting and anxiety. Even though the doctor had given me a clean bill of health and a little bottle of pills, which I took as prescribed, my headaches continued. In fact, the headaches plagued me for two years until I learned how to stop them before they started.

When I think of all I was trying to accomplish in a day's time, it's no wonder my head was signaling for me to slow down. My husband worked two jobs. I had three toddlers underfoot. And, there was housework, social commitments, and church volunteer work to do. I thoroughly enjoyed my responsibilities and busy life. I simply didn't realize the toll it was taking.

The cure? I became pregnant! Pregnant? This was something I certainly hadn't expected or dreamed would help get rid of the headaches. But in my seventh month, I used the pregnancy as an excuse to cancel all unnecessary activities and stay at home, resting. Very soon, the headaches began to subside.

After our baby was born, I stayed home and took the time to truly enjoy her. I didn't plan any parties and I eliminated most social functions. I was so happy living without that nagging headache, and my life was a joy. It was then that I realized I couldn't truly accomplish all I had in the past without paying a price. The price was stress and an accompanying headache.

The best way to handle a tension headache is to eliminate the cause before it starts. Instead of accepting a headache as a legitimate reason to be excused from duty, we should examine the priorities of our everyday lives. Headaches like mine can be a symptom of an external problem. The clinic couldn't tell me I was too busy. I had to figure that out for myself.

A humble woman voiced this splendid philosophy:

> *"When I works—I works hard:*
> *When I sits—I sits loose:*
> *When I worries—bless your heart,*
> *I just falls asleep."*

When I was growing up, the word *stress* was never used. Sundays were boring, to say the least. We kids were sent to Sunday School by parents who wanted to get us out of their hair for the morning. My sisters and I were so naïve. The thought never crossed our minds *why* my parents would want to be alone. We always wondered why they looked so happy when we came home. We spent the rest of the day on the front porch or visiting with neighbors.

As kids, we spent a lot of time outside. Our legs were used to get us to just about any place we wanted to go, and that eliminated any kind of stress behind the wheel of a car. We did not spend hours glued to the TV or computer.

Even now, when I feel I could use a break, if it isn't possible to go outside, I simply step to a window for a few minutes and look at the beautiful wide, wide world out there. Cloud formations, for example, have always fascinated and calmed me. Problems become insignificant and I am able to put everything in its proper perspective.

In those days, there were no shopping malls open on Sundays. In fact, there were no shopping malls at all. During those post-Depression days, we had no money to spend even if the stores had been open. We rested on Sundays.

Back then, we never heard the expression "all stressed out." Even today with all our modern, labor-saving devices, we have not found the time to truly relax. I believe we even need to rest after vacations!

In today's society, we are tempted to fill every minute of every day, almost feeling guilty if we have an idle moment. But the purpose of resting is to renew and restore our minds, as well as our bodies. When you use and honor these expressions, you will probably have a clearer, stress-relieving solution to your problem that will prevent you from becoming overly busy:

Let me sleep on it
Give me a little time.
Wait a while and I'll let you know later.
I want to relax a minute first.

The human body is made for six days of work and one day of rest. We short-circuit our whole being when we deny ourselves this one special treat—rest.

Sign in a Bagel Shop:

"Don't take life so seriously. You'll never get out of it alive!"

Falling Down

No one likes to imagine him- or herself lying on the ground, twisted like a pretzel because of some fluke accident that sends him or her sprawling along in the most ungraceful arrangement of limbs and backside. One night when I left the house for an evening out, I certainly never expected to fall—but then nobody does. Falls are, for the most part, always unexpected.

Don't ask me how, I still don't know, but I slipped on my daughter's driveway and landed in a ridiculous heap. Everything on me hurt; every muscle between my neck and my hips seemed to be sprained or strained. It was especially painful getting out of bed or rising from a chair. A paramedic taught me to push on the top of my knees to boost myself up to a standing position, but once again, after two days of struggling, the family said, "Go to the doctor!"

My daughter took me to her chiropractor who ordered X-rays and sort of massaged and comforted me. Then he said something all doctors should say to their patients, "You will get better."

What a powerful statement! Those words instilled such hope in me. I knew if I struggled along, eventually I'd be feeling good again. It was a long month filled with stabbing pains, limited movement, and restless sleep, but sure enough, just like the doctor said, I did get better. The Lord made our bodies to heal themselves when we give them time.

Has a doctor ever told you those inspiring words, "You will get better"?

Sometimes we are fortunate and we don't get hurt when we fall. As I was leaving church one Easter morning, all dressed up in my pretty yellow suit, we were heading toward the parking lot with the rest of my family when suddenly I tripped. I stumbled and fell over something jutting out of the sidewalk.

My granddaughter attracted a lot of attention when she yelled excitedly, "Grandma, are you all right?"

"Of course, I'm all right," I calmly reassured her. And the truth is, I was, although I made quite a spectacle of myself splattered all over the sidewalk where I just sort of rolled. I'd always heard that if you roll when you fall, you won't get hurt. Athletes are taught to do just that.

Onlookers parading out of church were surprised when I got up quickly, smiled, straightened my skirt, greeted everyone with a "Happy Easter," and continued to the car. Then we all laughed at the spectacle I'd made of myself. I didn't even have a run in my nylons!

Some Hard of Hearing Humor

During one particular hospital stay, I was amazed by how well I could hear. Hospitals are especially difficult places to hear because everyone tends to speak in hushed tones. Any time I am in a hospital, I always have to ask people to repeat themselves. But this time I had no trouble at all. Because of the deep incisions from my hysterectomy and appendectomy, I rarely left my bed during that stay. For a few days, my normal hearing returned. I thought that this was unbelievable. I had a hysterectomy and my hearing gets better!

On the fifth day, as I was sitting in a chair at the end of my bed, I read a large sign that said "HARD OF HEARING" which had been set by my chart. Disillusioned and embarrassed, I actually took my robe and covered the sign. Just then, I noticed a doctor who wore a prosthesis happily trotting down the hallway with his tell-tale limp. Recognizing how he handled his problem, I hastily uncovered the sign and let all be known. I am always thankful for the many kind people who project their voices for me. Even with my hearing aid, I still need a little help.

Flushing the Problem Out

While wintering in Florida one year, my husband began having trouble hearing. A friend who was enjoying the sunshine around the pool with us suggested that perhaps he had a wax build-up in his ear. It had recently become very loud in our home because I had a hearing problem myself and we were both forced to shout at each other in order to be heard. We decided to search the yellow pages for an ear, nose, and throat doctor, professionally known as an *otorhinolaryngologist*.

When you break the term down, *oto* refers to the ear; *rhino*, the nose; *laryn*, the throat, and the *ologist* part means you're going to pay a lot of money.

We found a name and an appointment was confirmed. The next day we found ourselves in the doctor's waiting room with the rest of the patients, waiting patiently for my husband's name to be called. The place was filled with *sick* people. Patients blew their noses, coughed into the open air (or more politely into a handkerchief); other patients glared at the rude coughers, looking up from their year-old magazines. Folks checked their watches and listened intently to the names being called, hoping desperately that the name would be their own.

Eventually, we were ushered into the inner office where the doctor finally appeared to greet us. He listened to my husband's complaint and after a brief examination of the ear, the doctor left the room.

A young intern entered next and began to follow the doctor's instructions to flush out the ear. A half-moon shaped cup was placed underneath and a syringe full of liquid was forced into my husband's ear. A moment or two later, the intern said, "Just look at all this wax I flushed out!"

I was seated on the only chair in the room, but when he said that, I jumped to my feet to have a look. There was nothing in that cup but clear water! Right then and there we should have insisted on seeing the doctor again. The intern then tried to suction the wax out, but to no avail. We walked out of that office knowing full well that all of the wax still remained in his ear. However, $110 was flushed out of my husband's wallet before we left.

We returned to our own medical doctor in Ohio. His nurse is a friend of ours and she advised us to buy a bottle of sweet oil, use it for three days to soften the wax, and then come back to the office to have the wax flushed out. Here's a news flash: Sweet oil is just olive oil. Read it on the label. It says *olive oil*. To our great relief three days later, the wax was easily flushed out after it was softened. We were amazed and relieved when his hearing returned to normal. No more shouting!

We have, since then, purchased an over-the-counter ear wax removal system. It's best to do it yourself; that way you can feel how much pressure is needed to flush out the ear without damaging the eardrum. I find that ear drops containing a fresh solution of Carbamide Peroxide will give the best results.

Later, after my husband had a hearing aid mold fitted, some wax pressed against a nerve in his ear and he became extremely dizzy and sick to his stomach. He didn't know he was suffering from an inner ear imbalance. He thought that he was dying. It happened about a week after the fitting, so he wasn't able to connect the dizziness with his hearing aid. The doctor solved the problem immediately by flushing out his ear. The dizziness stopped and my husband was happy. He wasn't dying after all.

Is That What He Really Said?

Since my husband and I now both wear hearing aids, we know how poor hearing can lead to a variety of predicaments. One afternoon, I made an appointment with my doctor because I had some pain around my heart. Naturally, I thought I was going to die, or at least I would need open heart surgery. I made myself a cup of hot tea to relax myself. (Incidentally, I've always thought hot tea is capable of solving many ailments.)

After the doctor examined me, he immediately ruled out any heart problems, but he sent me to the hospital for an examination anyway. I thought I'd heard him say that they were just going to do the "bare essentials." What he'd actually said was the "barium swallows."

When I arrived at the hospital, I was given some awful pink, chalky stuff to drink, and then I was escorted to the X-ray department where I waited for the stuff to go down.

It turned out that my problem was quite simple. The doctor explained to me during my next visit, "You have a nervous stomach."

"But I'm not the nervous type," I argued.

"Maybe not, but your stomach is." I told him about drinking hot tea for relaxation. "That's about the worst thing you can do for a nervous stomach," was his reply.

With that pronouncement, he handed me a prescription for a relaxation drug. Then he explained that there is a valve that comes out of the stomach near the heart, hence my great concern. I only needed about four of those pills and then the pain stopped, and so did the anxiety.

I'm not shy about asking any doctor to repeat himself until I fully understand what he is saying. Good hearing or not, good understanding is essential for good treatment. Once again, this had all happened while I'd been in a surgeon's office. I think that a family practitioner would have given me the pills first, and then if that medicine hadn't worked, other options would have been considered.

My hearing problem has to do with my eardrum. Although I wear a hearing aid, I still have difficulty hearing certain soft voices, whispers, and soft tones. It amazes me how well I can hear while driving in the mountains, or while I'm in a plane where the eardrum tightens and as we call it, *pops*. Some people complain while flying, and their ears pain them, but I sure wish there was a way for my eardrums to be repaired somehow. Apparently, a graft on my eardrum has stretched, causing the hearing loss.

I'm still very thankful for the hearing I have with the use of a hearing aid. I love to hear birds sing. I also appreciate my unique ability to turn off the noise whenever I choose to live in a quiet, peaceful world.

Is That What She Really Said?

Once a year, our family used to take a boat trip to visit my grandmother who lived on a lake island. Her home had no electricity or running water. It was just like going back a century in time, but oh how we loved it. Carrying a coal oil lamp up the stairway at night and watching the shadows on the wall, carrying in wood for the cook-stove to fry the pancakes for breakfast, dipping water from the rain barrel to water her garden, and picking her strawberries for her to sell gave us memories we'll never forget.

One day after lunch, Grandmother said in her soft, sweet voice, "Merle Jean, I want you to empty the tea pot." (My name is Muriel. She was the only one who called me Merle Jean.)

Because I did not hear her correctly, I went upstairs to empty the chamber jar, thinking all the while, emptying a pot is a terrible job to give a little child.

I knew that she never referred to the pot upstairs as the *pee pot*. It was always the *chamber jar*. It was later, when she asked me why I hadn't emptied the *tea pot*, that I learned to laugh at my hearing mistakes. Believe me, there have been many!

The Belly Laugh

A belly laugh is so healthy, especially when you are able to laugh at yourself. Every year I go along with friends to the South Florida Palm Beach County Fair. I don't particularly care for most of the activities, but it is a wonderful opportunity to enjoy one of those greasy sausage and onion sandwiches.

When we entered the main auditorium, it wasn't for the purpose of listening to the rock band that was playing at the time. We were there to see the act that would be following them. We decided to listen while we waited and rest our weary feet. A rock band performance is definitely not one of my favorite things, but I found myself beginning to enjoy the loud, ear-splitting music and the enthusiastic screams of the young people who really appreciated it. (We'll never know how much damage is done to their eardrums with the sound so greatly amplified.)

I asked my friend who was seated next to me, "When was the last time you screamed?"

"I don't even know if I can scream," was her reply.

She heartily agreed to my next suggestion, "Let's both scream as loud as we can with the rest of the kids when this next song is over."

My friend and I amazed ourselves by how loud we could scream. Nobody else screamed. We were so embarrassed we felt like crawling under our chairs. The crowd roared with laughter. Well, what are you going to do when you make a dumb mistake like that? You just sit there and grin and bear it. But later, we enjoyed a great big belly laugh.

"A merry heart doeth good like a medicine."
Proverbs 17:22

Healing a Heel Spur

On a routine visit with my family doctor, I mentioned how badly my heel hurt when I first got out of bed in the morning. He looked at my foot and carefully examined my heel.

"In my opinion," he said, "you have a heel spur."

He didn't order an X-ray, nor did he tell me how long it would take for a heel spur to go away. It always seems to me like older doctors just instinctively know what's wrong and what to do about it. He advised me to take two pans and put ice cold water in one, and very hot water in the other. He told me to dunk my foot first in the very hot water, and then in the icy water. I followed his advice and I soon felt a difference in the way my foot felt first thing in the morning. What he neglected to tell me was that it would take a year of patience for the heel spur to heal completely. There was still a nagging pain, but by walking on the outside of my foot, I managed to get around pretty well.

While playing golf, it became more irritated, however, so my daughter said those four familiar words, "Go to the doctor."

I followed her direction. As I was wintering in Florida, I decided to visit the podiatrist's office that we passed each morning on our way to the bagel shop. His sign, etched in the glass of the office window read "PODIATRIST," with the words "Foot Doctor" underneath. (I imagine that was for all us ignoramuses who don't know what a podiatrist is.) As I waited with the rest of the patients, I read a large poster from the Mayo Clinic that stated:

> Heel spurs are a bone calcification and heal themselves naturally in about a year. The calcification eventually dissolves into the blood stream.

Why wasn't I smart enough to believe what I read? Why didn't I walk out and go home? Who knows? After waiting for an eternity in the examining room, the doctor finally burst in, introduced himself, examined my foot briefly, and ordered an X-ray. Wait in the waiting room, wait in the examining room, and now wait for the X-rays to be developed. Wait, Wait, Wait!

After he looked at the X-ray, the doctor said, "You have a heel spur." (As if I didn't know.) "Would you like for me to give you a shot?" He appeared to have a snicker on his fact that suggested to me that the shot would be painful.

He did not explain what was in the *shot*, or what it would accomplish; nor did I ask how the shot could help. I gave a very short answer, "No."

I found out later that the cortisone shot would have broken up the calcification, helping it to heal more quickly. If he had explained that to me, I no doubt would have consented.

The doctor taped *both* of my feet—not together, of course—with lots of wide tape, and charged me $120. I went home and took that uncomfortable tape off in the middle of the night and decided to let nature take its course. How long was I supposed to wear that tape? The doctor never said a word about it! An expression my uncle used to use, "Useless as teats on a boar," seemed appropriate.

I tried using lifts and pads in my shoe, which were sold in the drugstore. They didn't help at all. Then I discovered my old Bass sandals, the thong type with no heel strap. They had a concave curve in the middle of the heel. At last, my foot felt comfortable, as the sandal did not allow any pressure on the bottom of my heel where the spur was located.

There were times I thought I would have to put up with that painful heel spur forever. My family doctor helped me handle the pain with the hot and cold water, but he never told me that my foot would get better. I was glad my foot healed before the cold weather came; you can't wear socks with thongs!

I thought if I saw a specialist, he would *do* something about it. I thought that with a professional diagnosis, there would be a cure. If the podiatrist had done a better job of explaining exactly how a cortisone shot worked, or if I had asked, the recovery process would have been shorter

The best advice turned out to be from that Mayo Clinic poster: *Heel spurs will heal themselves in about a year.* That's just about how long it took. Now I tend to think of informational notices in waiting rooms as something like manufacturers' recipes on the back of food packages. They are usually the best, and they are free.

Discretion, Please!

What's a Sigmoid?

My husband and I felt really good, so it didn't seem necessary to schedule an appointment for our annual physicals with our family doctor. We like him a lot, though, as do many of his other patients. His office walls are covered with thank-you cards and scrawled notes of praise. I always figured that if I didn't go to the doctor, he wouldn't find anything wrong with me. I knew that wasn't very good logic at my age, so I went, and I dragged my husband with me, because he never wants to go either.

After my examination, I was instructed to wait while the doctor did a routine prostate examination on my husband. I was surprised when the doctor called me into his office, and with my husband seated next to me, told us that he had discovered something that was reason enough to schedule an appointment with a proctologist. (For lack of a better definition, that's the guy who examines the plumbing.)

During our first visit with the proctologist, he recommended a *sigmoid*. I didn't understand him clearly, so I asked the nurse at the front desk. She explained how doctors usually shorten the official terminology to *sigmoid*, and seldom bothers to even pronounce the "d" at the end of the word. He was, it turns out, referring to a test called a *sigmoidoscopy*. She wrote it down so I could both spell and pronounce it. The examination was performed by inserting a tiny camera to locate anything unusual in the colon.

Farm folks like my husband are not the least bit embarrassed to talk about any part of the anatomy, and he soon discovered many of the men around the condo complex we lived in had been through the same type of procedure. My husband wasn't too concerned about it being anything serious. He simply blamed it on all that strawberry jam he eats for breakfast every morning.

When the day finally came for the 11:00 a.m. appointment with the proctologist, he was up much earlier than usual, wondering how to use the little bottle containing water for his Fleet enema. It was a new experience for him. He brought it into the kitchen, read the directions on the box, and placed the little bottle on the counter while he read the morning paper. Well, I wasn't about to make my toast with that thing sitting there staring at me, so I put it in the bathroom where it belonged.

Meet Mr. Anxiety! The office was 15 minutes away, and we left home at 10:00 a.m. for the 11:00 appointment, only to be greeted by 26 people in the waiting room. Seeing all those patients overwhelmed us. The last time we'd been there, we'd been the only ones. When we learned that there were six other doctors sharing the office space, my husband began to relax a bit, but he exhibited his impatience by jumping to his feet frequently and striding to the desk to make sure that he was not going to be overlooked. At last, at 11:27, he was summoned into the doctor's examination room.

I had the comfort of waiting while the doctor examined him. This time was whiled away watching all of the other patients streaming in and out of this busy place. It resembled an airport, with comfortable seats, two televisions, and lots of reading material—enough for a library.

A woman behind a newspaper remained invisible. Another woman walked out wearing a pair of old pedal pushers, just like mine (the kind I wouldn't wear to a dog fight), while another extremely sharp gal strolled in wearing black spandex with a gold belt. She took the prize for the day as far as fashion went. A man with black socks and white sneakers, a man wearing a black hat emblazoned with NYFD and a bright yellow shirt, and a man with a long neck and bulging eyes who reminded me of a turkey, were all watching TV. A small child was taking a nap on her mother's lap, and she, too, fell asleep, leaving me to wonder how long she had been waiting. A nice gentleman with a sportswatch, who checked it often, sat next to a man in the plaid shirt who leaned on his walker. My heart went out to this man. He looked so worried and so alone.

I anxiously waited to see the expression on my husband's face after his examination, but instead, I heard my own name called and I was ushered into the examination room. My husband's rather bewildered look gave me an indication that all was not well. The doctor pointed to a chart depicting the location of a polyp in his colon.

The doctor said, reassuringly, "It's a very small polyp, but we'll need to do a colonoscopy."

"Is that just an examination, or is there surgery involved, too?" my husband questioned.

"We'll take care of the polyp at the same time. This is quite common among older men," the doctor replied.

My husband was clearly beginning to feel older by the minute. We obediently returned to the front desk where a nurse scheduled the necessary procedure for the following Tuesday. At least the word *colonoscopy* was a little easier to pronounce than *sigmoidoscopy.*

A week of waiting seemed to my husband like a year's worth of minutes. On Sunday evening, I suggested he take a dip in the pool. I sat on the edge, dangling my feet in the water. It was a lovely evening—too nice outside to sit in the house and fret.

Two friends, Bill and Tony, climbed into the pool and excitedly described all the fish they had caught the day before in Key West. It wasn't two minutes before my husband changed the subject and brought up his colonoscopy. He started right in, "Tomorrow's the big day."

Then, the teasing began. Tony remarked, "You better get yourself some powder puffs!"

Bill added, "When I had mine, I was given this powdery stuff to mix with a gallon of water. I had to drink a glass of it, and then another, and then another, all day long!"

"I'm only supposed to drink three ounces of some Fleet mixture," the future patient protested.

"Well," Tony said, "if you don't get yourself cleaned out, they won't do it, and you'll be sent home."

"I always drink lots of water," my husband replied. "But I still don't understand how the doctor can get rid of the polyp."

Tony's jaw dropped. "You only have one? Mine was the size of a golf ball!"

Bill seemed to relish the thought of explaining exactly how it's done. "First, they run this long, nine foot hose in…"

"Hey! Wait a minute!" my husband gasped. "I'm only five foot nine myself!"

Tony reached over and removed my sunglasses, then placed them on my husband's face. "That's the way you'll come out of the office, because they take a piece of your eyes, too, with that big long hose. It's a real 'crappy' job." He winked at me. "You've watched them stuff a sausage, haven't you?" His comments were illustrated by a circle made with thumb and finger.

Bill took over. "The whole thing is blown up when they pump air into you."

My husband looked down and shook his head. "Oh, the poor doctor. When I was lying on the table, I felt the rumbling. I knew I couldn't hold back the gas, and I warned him, 'I think I have to go to the bathroom,' but it was too late."

Tony whispered, "I know, the whole thing's a shitty mess."

"I still can't understand how the doctor can see what he's doing." My dear mate just wasn't going to let this thing go.

Bill explained, "There's a little camera in the tube. And the doctor uses those scissors with the long handles in there, too."

"But wouldn't that cut the tube?"

"Sure, but then it's over and they pull the tube out."

"And make sure they put you to sleep and give you something for pain," Tony added.

"Nah, he'll miss everything if he's out," Bill retorted.

Tony waved him off with a laugh. "Now, let's hear you pronounce it."

Job's friends could have done a better job of psyching my husband up for this common procedure.

On Monday, my husband said, "Tomorrow at this time, I'll be on the table."

Half an hour later, he informed me, "I'm turning down the air conditioner."

My husband reread the instructions from the doctor for the fourth time. One and a half ounces of the Fleet mixture were to be mixed in a clear liquid, followed by a whole glass of water. Very simple. After doing so, he lay down, waiting to see what would happen next.

I knew he had success when he yelled out the door to Tony, "The fleet's in!"

We promptly arrived at the outpatient clinic at 6:15 a.m. All the staff were very pleasant and helpful. We were pleased by how efficiently and smoothly everything was carried out. My only complaint was the 60-degree temperature in the waiting room. Because my husband was anesthetized, he had no complaints at all. In less than two hours, he was wheeled into the waiting room with a big smile on his face, waving his discharge and instruction papers.

"Well, how did it go?" I asked.

"A piece of cake," he replied with a smile.

On the way home he said, "I still don't know how the doctor did it."

The Bedpan

This is not a pleasant subject. I don't know of anyone who looks forward to using a bedpan. Just the mention of one makes people squirm with feelings of distress and embarrassment. The few times it was necessary for me to use the bedpan were the only times I wished I was a man.

During one of my hospital stays, my roommate, the patient in Bed B, was recovering from knee surgery. Because the curtain between our beds was drawn, I didn't notice when the nurse put her on the bedpan.

I was wondering what in the world was going on behind that drawn curtain that would make a patient make such odd sounds. She seemed to be mumbling some four-letter words.

Finally, she blurted out, "I can't go on this d--- thing!"

The position she was forced into was causing her knee a great deal of pain, which added to her frustration that she was unable to make a contribution to the bedpan. I felt so sorry for her.

After listening to her fussing for a few more minutes, I jumped to my feet, very thankful that I could get up and not be in her predicament. I took two pieces of paper towel, folded them into a pad, soaked them with hot water, then gently moved the curtain aside just far enough to slide my hand through and handed her the hot, wet paper.

"Try placing this warm pad down there," I offered.

I could hear. She had immediate success.

"Oh, thank you so much," she said with relief. "Where did you learn that trick?"

When I tried to think, I really couldn't remember, but it sure worked for her. Unfortunately, filling the bedpan was only part of her problem. Because of her knee pain, getting off the bedpan was just as difficult. She would ring for the nurse and wait and wait, and then she would ring again. It was most uncomfortable for her to lie like that for a long time, unable to boost herself off the bedpan.

"Let me try my call button, too, and let's see if that catches the nurses' attention," I volunteered. We waited another 20 minutes.

"This is ridiculous. Why don't they come?" she asked in disgust.

Finally, I got up and removed the bedpan myself. I covered it with a towel until it was emptied. She was very grateful. We both learned the hard way, that bedpan detail has no priority at the nurses' station.

Later that day, she confided in her physical therapist who understood her anguish and evidently corrected the situation. The next time she used the bedpan, the nurse didn't even leave the room until she was finished, whereupon it was promptly removed.

This is just one example of the needless suffering patients endure. After all, patients, as customers, are paying for any and all services rendered by the hospital staff, including this necessary duty. Patients very seldom think of themselves as customers, nor do nurses like to think of themselves as service providers. Rather, the medical profession dictates the care of patients—giving them little, if any, *rights*—and charges them dearly for doing so.

The D and C

I hadn't the slightest notion what the D or the C stood for when my gynecologist suggested that I have one. I know now; it stands for *Dilation* and *Curettage*, and it's definitely female-related.

This was to be my very first time in a hospital for anything other than giving birth. My youngest child was almost 20 years old, but just the same, a scary feeling gripped me as I walked up to the admitting desk—the same kind of fear that produces sweaty palms.

I was admitted at about 1:00 p.m. The last time I'd been in a wheelchair, a baby was in my arms as they wheeled me out the door. Now, I found myself being wheeled into a hospital room. They did let me walk to the X-ray department, and to the lab for the necessary blood work, though. I was a quite apprehensive, not knowing what would happen next.

Well, the fact is, nothing happened! I waited in my room all afternoon until well after the evening meal was served. I received the customary visit from the doctor who was scheduled to do the surgery, and he seemed very friendly. Actually, he was just killing time. One of his patients was in labor and he was waiting to be summoned to deliver the baby. He did not explain anything to me, nor did I have the presence of mind to ask. As I learned later, the D and C procedure is very simple and very common.

After a poor night of rest because of all the noise and light, I got up, bathed, and hopped back into bed to wait some more. Then I saw that big needle coming at me. A nurse came in with a breakfast tray, but when she realized she was in the wrong room, she quickly whisked away what I thought was my breakfast. I was nervous and hungry, and I almost cried when they took away my morning coffee. Instead, I got a shot to make me relax. I relaxed, all right. I had no recollection of being transported to the operating room, of seeing any doctors or nurses, of the gurney ride back to my room, or being rolled back into bed.

At noon, a nurse gently touched my arm and suggested, "I think it's about time for you to wake up and eat your lunch."

"Oh, no," I replied, "I can't eat anything before my surgery."

"Honey, you done already had that surgery." This nurse called everyone "honey." I liked her.

I don't wake up too easily. When the nurse left, I sat up and turned my legs over the side of the bed where they dangled for a while. While coming to my senses, I realized that I was in a hospital and I was hungry. With great anticipation, I removed the cover of my entrée only to discover *Johnny Marzetti*. Did I really expect filet mignon? Or lobster bisque? Or stuffed clams in a white sauce? Ask any kid in grade school who eats in the school cafeteria, and he will tell you about Johnny Marzetti. It's overcooked macaroni and ground meat in a tomato sauce. My mom used to call this dish *scrambled hamburg*, and I have also heard it referred to as *slumgullion*. It sounds like it was borne of the Depression. I never liked it, and apparently the person who named it slumgullion didn't like it either. I hadn't eaten any breakfast though, and since there was no one interested in my complaint, I went ahead and ate it anyway.

The meal was topped off with a chocolate and lemon pudding for dessert. Tomato, chocolate, and lemon: my taste buds said, "No way." I passed on the dessert, thinking that hospital dietitians must think we have cast-iron stomachs. I wondered if they ate the same things they dished out for the patients.

I was allowed to choose from a menu for the evening meal. Everything was served in small dishes, covered with warming lids. There was nothing green or fresh, except a piece of kale intended as garnish. The ward nurse who picked up the dinner trays couldn't believe I had eaten the kale.

Another sleepless night followed. It never occurred to me to ask for a sleeping pill. The lady in Bed B snored very loudly, the illumination from the hall lights made it seem as though night had never come, and by morning, I was more than ready to go home. I packed my few items and waited patiently for the doctor to release me. Why that took so long, I don't know. Perhaps he was delivering another baby. Finally, he sent word to the desk that I was to be discharged.

It wasn't necessary for me to spend the whole day in bed the day before the surgery, and I am very thankful the procedure was performed under anesthetics. However, I could have rested and gone home the same day. Today, D and Cs are performed on an outpatient basis, and I think that's just fine. This is one procedure where I agree wholeheartedly with the dictates of the insurance companies.

The Hemorrhoidectomy

This surgery was lots of fun. Ha! Although drinking all that horrible Castor Oil before the procedure may have been the worst part of it.

It seemed to be a rather slow day in the operating room. There were only two of us lying in that refrigerated room, waiting for our gurneys to be rolled in. When the nurse felt my ice cold hand she knew that I wasn't kidding when I asked for a fourth warm blanket.

It is certainly a blessing that one doesn't recall much of what goes on in the operating room. I was pretty well drugged, therefore I don't have much memory of the operation, or of being transported and placed back into my bed. The doctor required me to stay in the hospital for seven days after the surgery.

During this hospital stay, I was fully aware of the fact that you need to *ask* for pain medication. I requested it to be given in hypo form, because it works quicker. I don't recall being too uncomfortable afterward. In fact, I don't recall feeling much of anything afterward. Perhaps being numb to the pain, I felt too well and energetic for my own good. I preferred visiting with a friend in the next room instead of resting in bed. I realized later that staying off my feet would have been more beneficial in allowing the swelling *down there* to decrease and return to normal.

I was advised to drink lots of water to get my plumbing working again. Not having success in the bathroom, I was subjected to the experience I'd always dreaded. Catheterization was not nearly as embarrassing or as unpleasant as I thought it would be. I lived.

One morning, I was awakened at 5:00 a.m. by a nurse's aide filling my water pitcher with ice. Ice is noisy. (As I write about this thoughtless deed, a nasty little voice in my head is saying, "If someone ever wakes me unnecessarily at 5:00 a.m. again, I'll take my arm and sweep that pitcher of ice onto the floor!")

I realized then that I was feeling intense pain for the first time since my operation. The effect of the shot I'd been given at 3:00 a.m.

had worn off. I knew better than to ask again. Five o'clock in the morning was not the time for me to ask for another shot. Directly across from my room was a bathroom with a huge bathtub. I tiptoed across the hall, sprinkled a little soap in the water to make a bubble bath, filled that big tub to the brim, and slid down deep into the nice hot water. I felt so rich. There is nothing like a warm water soak for pain. I became so relaxed that I fell asleep.

At 8:00 a.m., a nurse burst into the bathroom and declared, "So, there you are! We have been looking all over for you! Now get out of that tub and back into bed. It's time for breakfast." She ordered me around like I was a five-year-old.

She seemed quite perturbed that I would think for myself and not consult anyone about taking a bath. Of course, from her standpoint, she was probably wondering how she was going to explain a missing patient. By now, the tub water was only lukewarm, so I gladly retreated to my assigned room to devour my breakfast and request another pain shot.

I am thankful that I never seem to lose my appetite while recovering in a hospital. Breakfast, by far, seems to be the most appetizing of the meals served. It's fun to lift those lids off the hot cereal, pour on the cream, drink the variety of juices, butter the toast, and relax with my morning coffee. Doesn't that sound inviting? Someone else does the dishes—another plus!

This surgery took place during a particularly cold January. Only gray skies were visible out my north window. Hospital blankets are made of heavy washable cotton, and when I asked for yet another blanket, the nurse replied, "You have five blankets on that bed now!"

"But I'm still cold," I insisted.

I touched her arm with my cold hand, and she returned with another blanket. I was longing for the soft warm comforter I had on my bed at home. Under six heavy blankets, I could barely turn over.

The doctor was very understanding when I complained about being awakened unnecessarily at 5:00 a.m. by someone filling a water pitcher. I am sure that he had more important things on his mind than addressing the thoughtlessness of a nurse's aide, but he didn't make me feel like a tattletale, and it didn't happen again. After all, patients should have some rights, and one of those rights should be getting a good night's rest. Voicing your complaints or desires to the right person—often your own physician—is the key to success.

One evening, about the fourth day after this surgery, after the patient in Bed B had been dismissed, I was resting contentedly. Alone, I chose not to watch TV or to visit with anyone; instead, I chose to meditate in silence. My attention was drawn to a sweet bouquet of fresh-cut flowers that had been sent to me by my granddaughter. As my eyes lingered on them, every flower sprung to life. Each radiant blossom appeared to be filled with joy and seemed to be saying, "Come and dance with me!" A large white rose looked as if it was lifting its face to be kissed. I was thrilled to consider how these silent messengers of love had been blessed by their creator, and in turn had blessed me. I smiled. Hospitals can sometimes be a good place for thoughtful reflection and enjoyment when you look for it.

My doctor had warned me that the hemorrhoid surgery would not take care of my problem forever, and that hemorrhoids can reoccur. He did not advise me how to avoid them, nor was any instruction given to pay attention to diet. When I got home, I began reading my health books, and I read every chapter on how to prevent hemorrhoids.

Some books suggested that half of adults over the age of 40 suffer from hemorrhoids, which are simply varicose veins of the anal region. Strain can be caused by passing stool, which is the prime cause of preventing the blood from getting through to the larger veins. But straining also comes under circumstances not associated with a difficult bowel movement. Lifting a heavy object and even coughing tightens abdominal muscles, thereby squeezing on those veins and causing them to swell and sometimes bleed. It is important while lifting or straining to inhale and exhale constantly. (Observe weightlifters.) Never hold your breath while lifting.

Drink lots of water and juices. Avoid sugar and refined foods made of white flour. Hemorrhoids are virtually unknown in countries where foods are eaten in their natural state. Lots and lots of vegetables, especially dark green leafy ones, are suggested. The meat and potato guys won't be too happy about that, I suppose. Fresh vegetables are often recommended to maintain optimum health, because they are loaded with necessary minerals, vitamins, and roughage.

Foods rich in vitamin C, bioflavonoids, and vitamin E are essential—fresh raw fruits and vegetables, especially cabbage, green peppers, citrus fruits (including the white of the rind), rose hips, and black currants, along with whole grains, seeds, and nuts are especially good for you. As for me, I found that fresh pineapple or papaya work wonders. Taking vitamin B6 after each meal has been shown in some studies to affect speedy recovery. And give careful attention to cleanliness. These are the gleanings from a few of my health books.

You may find that doctors are not particularly nutrition-oriented. Consequently, the best thing to do is to educate yourself. Libraries and health food stores are stocked with many books that will help any one interested in developing a healthier diet. Your nether-regions will thank you for it.

The Mystery Rash

I have been blessed during my lifetime to have not one home, but two. My husband and I have wintered in south Florida each year for more than 20 years. Owning a residence in a southern climate also makes our place a vacation destination for our children, relatives, and friends. We often welcome with great joy visitors from afar, and I like to think that we act as something of a health sanitarium for our children and grandchildren who arrive with pale skin, sniffles, and gray circles under their eyes. Ten days later, they leave with rosy cheeks, sparkling eyes, and a spring in their step.

We have also had to deal with the common drawbacks of living in the tropics—sand spurs in the grass, fire ants, Palmetto bugs, sunburns, and stings from the Portuguese Man-of-War, or "blue bubbles," as we commonly refer to them.

Recently, after my daughter and her family returned to their home in the north, she called and told me about a strange rash her husband acquired while in Florida. It began under the hairline on the back of his neck and was spreading down his shoulders.

Figuring that a rash is not a serious condition, I sent her some creams and lotions I had used and offered my best advice, "Tell him not to scratch!"

My son-in-law happens to be one of those people who scratches a mosquito bite until it bleeds, so I'm sure that between his wife nagging him to quit scratching and the terrible urge to do so, he was being driven crazy.

The next week, they went to Cozumel, an island off the coast of Mexico. She called a few days after they returned to report that the rash was officially *on the move*. It had traveled under his arms, to his sides, and all around his bathing-suit lines. In short, he was in agony back at his computing job in New York City. He couldn't exactly scratch what itched because he was sitting on it!

His fishing buddy from Florida had apparently joked that, "If he would just wash his ass once a week, that would help!"

My daughter had scheduled an appointment with a dermatologist before they'd gone to Mexico, and he only had to wait one more week to see the doctor.

During that week, my daughter talked to both her family doctor and her pharmacist, she read all the medical books she had, and she researched rashes on the Internet. She thought it could possibly be poison ivy, except for the fact that the rash had been there for six weeks, and there were no tiny blisters; they were more like small welts. A cousin suggested he might have scabies, which are a type of skin lice that do itch like mad, and are also highly contagious. After their romantic trip to Mexico, my daughter was sure she would have contracted them, if that were the case. It could have been hives, but hives are an allergic reaction to something. She thought hard. Had they tried any new soap, cosmetics, or food recently? She couldn't think of anything.

Then, there was the new threat of *sea lice*. A relatively new beach pest had been found during the Spring along the gold coast of south Florida, as well as in Mexico. Sea lice are actually the larvae of thimble jellyfish that float invisibly in the ocean water and bury themselves in bathers' skin around the hairlines and bathing suits. Apparently, the rash doesn't last for long, unless someone becomes infested again, and then it itches like crazy.

When the day arrived for the visit to the dermatologist, my son-in-law was not expecting the doctor to be a woman! He was told to undress and stand on the end of the examination table. The doctor examined the scabs and patches of bumps that he had scratched so badly. They were difficult to diagnose. By now, the rash had moved to his hands and wrists (which is a tell-tale signs of scabies). The doctor looked puzzled, and asked, "Would you mind waiting a minute? I would like my partner to see this."

She left the room and soon returned with her male partner, who was also accompanied by a female intern. They all looked him over carefully.

The male doctor asked, "Is there any rash on your penis?"

My daughter watched the expression on her husband's face. He had, by now, become quite irritated—I think embarrassed would be an understatement—and he didn't think the doctor's request was necessary. At the same time, my daughter found the whole episode quite amusing.

He shook his head and said emphatically, "No."

The doctor persisted, "I think we had better take a look at your penis."

He swallowed hard while the underwear was pulled down and he watched in vain as the doctors' heads went this way and that.

"All clear there," they agreed.

The three of them backed up, spoke in hushed tones to each other, and then nodded their heads in agreement. Scabies was their diagnosis, though my daughter preferred to call it their "best guess." There were no scraping or samples sent to the lab, and no real evidence to back their assumption, but if all three doctors had come up with the same guess, it was deemed a professional diagnosis.

He was given a prescription for Lindane lotion, which was to be applied once from the neck down, and reapplied one week later. He used the medicine, but was still itching a month later, although not as much. Was it really scabies? Was it sea lice? Or some unknown rash? No one will ever know. After two months, the rash was gone and it doesn't really matter what it was. Many illnesses come and go, whether they are correctly diagnosed or not.

More important than treating the cause of the rash, or even getting rid of it, my son-in-law wanted a prescription for some serious anti-itch medicine, not just the over-the-counter stuff. But none was prescribed. That's why he'd scheduled the office visit in the first place, and he'd left quite discouraged and disappointed, feeling that he had wasted both his time and money.

Experienced dermatologists know that there are very few rashes that stick around forever. I guess it seemed best for the three of them to agree on some diagnosis, and to appear professional by prescribing a lotion, an over-the-counter one, at that.

Another Mystery Rash

(I love the way my granddaughter tells this story about a rash she had as a young girl.)

"When I was about 14 years old, I developed a skin rash. It started out being the size of a quarter, and by the time it was in its full glory, it resembled a map of the seven continents. The rash covered much of my thighs, forearms, face, and a small part of my calves. It had a raised red surface that, fortunately, never itched, but looked a little scaly.

"As good parents should, mine took me to the doctor. My dad usually took me because he had a more flexible work schedule. He took me again, and again, and again.

"Each time the doctor would say, 'I think we'll try something a little more powerful, or maybe less irritating, or maybe a lotion instead of the cream. That should do the trick.'

"We heard this over and over again. Is that what you call practicing medicine? By the end of the month, I had a small wicker basket filled with more than 30 different prescription creams. Lotrisone was the first cream used, but since the rash returned after I stopped applying it, the doctor felt it best to keep trying other medications that would get rid of the rash completely. This dermatologist would not prescribe more Lotrisone for me, even though none of the other creams had any effect whatsoever.

"After we exhausted this dermatologist's ideas, we decided to go for the big guns. Yes, we would take this mystery and present it to the good doctors in a well-known research clinic in a large city. I took part of the day off from school and my father and I started on our adventure.

"When we arrived, the nurse asked me to put on a paper dress in a partitioned part of the room. This was all new to me. Undressing for a dermatologist? I mean *everything* but my underwear. So there we were, a father and daughter, sitting two feet apart, he with his magazine, and me with nothing on but a thin paper dress and my underwear. I was feeling mighty uncomfortable, not knowing what to expect next.

"The doctor came in, followed by a fellow, who was followed by a resident, who was followed by two med students—all men.

There were now five men in the room, besides my father and me. Then we came to what I consider to be one of the scariest 10 minutes of my entire youth. While in the throngs of puberty, I had to show these six men my rash. And even worse, I had to expose the parts of my body where the rash was not. To this day, my father and I have never talked about the moment when they lowered the front of my gown, and there I was, naked in front of my father. It was almost enough to stunt puberty altogether. The doctor pulled back my underwear and let all those in the room look, so that they could 'confirm that the rash was not on her buttocks.'

"We began reviewing our family's skin history. When the doctors noticed my father's elbows and arms covered with psoriasis, they all came to a hasty conclusion. With no clinical tests or lab work, it was clear in all of their minds. This rash was psoriasis, even though the symptoms described were definitely not typical of psoriasis. (My rash never itched, there was none on my knees or elbows, and the rash did not respond to any of the treatments given me for psoriasis). Nonetheless, in their professional opinions, I definitely had psoriasis.

"The doctors were glad to hear about our upcoming Florida vacation. They said that nothing helps psoriasis more than salt water and sun.

"You have probably never witnessed a sight like that of my skin in Florida, however. The pinkish areas turned bright red. The slightly raised surface became extremely raised. These areas looked like pictures you might find in a geography book illustrating plateaus—those huge, flat, raised areas jutting out of the ground. They would have looked exactly like plateaus, if it hadn't been for all the pimples. Please take me literally. I am not embellishing when I say that every pore within the rash area was a full-scale, ready-to-burst pimple. When I attended to some, they came back within the hour. It was horrible. I was 14 years old, and there is no other word for it. Horrible!

"Now I knew the situation was bad. I could see the problem in my mirror. I could see the way strangers looked at me. But the true magnitude of the problem was brought to my attention when, on one Sunday, my mother said, 'Honey, you don't have to go to church today.'

"If my mom ever had a soapbox, it was while we were in Florida. On it, she preached with the best of them that her kids *do* go to church on vacation, and they *do not* complain. I didn't even think to ask about not attending church! But now, my own mother thought that my skin looked so bad, she encouraged me to skip the Easter story. Now that, my friends, is B-A-D, bad!

"My mystery rash calmed down after we returned to Ohio. We were especially glad to know for sure that the rash was not psoriasis. My parents took me to our family doctor and begged him to prescribe Lotrisone, which we knew had worked the best. He obliged, and wrote a prescription for the drug, and in an anti-climactic way, after using the cream, the rash fizzled into nonexistence. Every now and then over the years, I see a dime-sized spot for a day or two, but it always seems to go away uneventfully."

Hospitals: How to Survive Them

Doctors and Patients

We are fortunate in this country to have access to excellent health care. However, when you think about it, doctors are still just *practicing* medicine—practice, as in "let's try this," or "it could be that," or, "I seem to recall a former patient who had many of these symptoms."

> *"Beware of the young doctor and the old barber.*
> *God heals and the doctor takes the fee."*

> —Benjamin Franklin

Medical arts practitioner is a more appropriate term for doctors, I believe. Let's face it: Medicine is more of an art than a science. Today's technical approach to everything leads one to believe that once a diagnosis has been made, there is a scientifically proven path to a cure. But it isn't true. Symptoms can vary for each person, depending on everything from age and sex, to weight and physical activity level.

Even within one's own family, each body and the way it reacts to treatment is unique and, many times, inconsistent. Man is so much more than dust inhabited by life.

His soul, his intellect, his spirituality, his upbringing, and his determination to live are all represented in his physical health. The human body is truly an amazingly intricate, complex creation. Doctors try their best to pinpoint and accurately diagnose problems, but honest mistakes are made every day.

On the other side of the coin, whose job is it to inform the doctor? Patients don't always do the best job explaining their condition to the doctor either, many times exaggerating or minimizing their often complex ailments. Going to the doctor is somewhat like taking a car to a repair shop. One has to do a good job explaining the problem, including mimicking the noises, for a mechanic to properly diagnose the problem. Having a physician who will discard preconceived ideas and truly listen to our ailments helps the most. Clear communication is one of the keys to maintaining quality health care.

What do we really expect a doctor to do for us when we go to his or her office? Prescribe a drug? Give us a shot? Send us to the hospital for tests, or refer us to a surgeon? In general, make us better? Sometimes, upon examination, the doctor will simply give us his professional opinion. The condition or pain that brought us to his office is nothing to worry about. "It's healing nicely." That's the kind of visit I like most. It's almost as good as hearing the doctor say, "You'll get better." And sometimes that advice, that wisdom that he shares, is priceless. But most of the time, we expect the doctor to *do* something.

That's the time to do your homework. Find out as much as you can about your problem or condition before you see the doctor for his opinion or treatment. There are many ways to learn about health, medicine, and treatments for various conditions. I have gleaned information from patients and doctors, schools and teachers, books and the media, but where I learned the most was from my own mistakes. I have learned by making mistakes myself as a patient, and I have also benefited from the mistakes made by friends, family, acquaintances, or fellow patients I meet while waiting patiently in doctors' offices.

Maybe that's why doctors call their customers "patients." One of the definitions a dictionary gives for patient is: calmly tolerating delay, confusion or inefficiency; bearing or enduring pain, trouble, or anxiety without complaining or losing self-control or making a disturbance.

On the other hand, maybe that's not the reason. All I know is that I have endured my share of waiting as a patient, and I tend to believe that much of the suffering and frustration that comes with being a patient could be avoided if we weren't asked to wait so long. Sometimes you just have to speak up!

You would think we would be used to waiting. We wait in line to use the restroom, at reservation desks in airports, in front of red lights, for mail deliveries, to be seated in a restaurant or theater, and we wait for our eggs to boil. But when our health is concerned, we wish there would be no waiting. It's "Hurry up, doctor. I feel lousy. Do something quick to help me get better!"

The Calcified Tendon

The following is a description of my treatment for a calcified tendon I had in my arm, and the predicament I found myself in when trying to console another patient.

An orthopedic doctor hospitalized me because of extreme pain in my arm. I didn't know why my arm was so stiff and painful, and neither did he. Needless to say, the X-rays taken should have revealed the calcified tendons, but were overlooked either by the radiologist or the doctor, or both. Nobody is admitted to the hospital today with a calcified tendon.

53

While in the hospital, I endured useless, painful therapy for a number of days. Every day, I found myself riding in a wheelchair on my way to the therapy room, even though I was perfectly capable of walking. After all, there was nothing wrong with my legs, and I could have benefited from the exercise.

The determined therapist gave me an object that resembled a sawed-off broomstick and I was ordered to take hold of it with both hands and raise it above my head. I put forth my best effort, but my poor aching arm would not go up. I watched both of the therapist's eyebrows rise as she coached me with a positive but demanding attitude. I was amazed myself that my arm didn't respond to this aggressive therapist. After the therapy session was over, I was placed in the hall in my wheelchair where I waited until one of those nice volunteers pushed my wheelchair to my room and I rested until the next therapy session.

Volunteers are lovely people who fill their days with good deeds such as pushing patients in wheelchairs, offering reading material, and sometimes stopping by each room to greet patients with a cheery hello and a smile.

One day I awoke from a nap. A new woman had been assigned to the bed next to mine. When I rolled over, I saw two of the largest knees I had ever seen in my life. This woman weighed 525 pounds, at least. She had been admitted for a D and C, but first, she needed to get her blood pressure down so that this simple surgery wouldn't be life threatening.

As we ate our evening meal together, she shared many sad things about her life. Her twin babies had died several years ago and she related to me how overcome with grief she and her husband had become. I sincerely expressed my sympathy to her, realizing that many times when someone is grieving over such a tremendous loss, they turn to excessive eating.

I asked her, "Is that when you let yourself get so heavy?"

I thought I was being careful, not using the word *fat*. Instead, I was in big trouble. The woman became very disturbed and stopped eating. She was having a bad day and she didn't need any advice from me, especially after I had made that thoughtless remark.

I tried to correct my thoughtless blunder, but only compounded the problem by quoting a pro-football player who I'd heard say, "I could live on my own body weight for a week."

This football player was a lean, trim, strong, muscular hunk of a man who didn't have an ounce of fat on him, leaving no room for comparison to an overweight woman. Next thing you know, her blood pressure shot way up and I was asked by a nurse to leave the room. Not only that, they planned to assign me to another room!

As soon as I learned why she was so angry and upset, I went to her tearfully and apologized as sincerely as possible. I told her how sorry I was that I had offended her, and that it certainly hadn't been my intention.

Later, the nurse said, "I think it will be okay for you to come back into your room."

Thanks a lot! I didn't say it out loud. I just thought it. I guess she didn't think I would cause any more problems.

Many overweight people take on a jolly disposition to detract attention from their weight, but this woman had a sad and bitter manner about her. Her reaction to my question about her weight had revealed to me that she thought I was cruel, when in actuality, I was only trying to get her to confide in me. Perhaps I could help her. I had no idea that my question would make her so upset and angry. I wondered to myself, why in the world wouldn't her doctor put her on a diet? I was very careful from that point on to avoid any topic of conversation that would offend her, like food.

I was released from the hospital nine days later with the same amount of pain in my arm as I'd had when I was admitted. I still didn't know what was wrong. I suffered with that calcified tendon for another month, until a friend of mine advised me to go to his doctor who had cured a similar problem he had.

Once again, we see the value of comparing ailments. More X-rays were ordered, and this time the calcification was discovered in my arm, just above the elbow. I was given a couple of shots of cortisone, which broke up the calcification, and about three weeks later, my arm was completely free of pain.

Getting to sleep at night with pain was terribly difficult for me, so occasionally I would take a nap during the day. I remember it like it was yesterday. I was watching a World Series game when I fell asleep with the heating pad on my arm. When I awoke, the pain was gone—I mean *all* gone—and it never returned. Plus, our team won the ball game. What a great day!

A saying seen on a doctor's wall:

"Happy is the day when you awake without pain."

The first doctor I consulted before going to the hospital gave me a series of cortisone shots in the bursa on the top of the arm. When the shots had no effect, he said there was nothing more he could do for me. The second doctor X-rayed my arm and put me in the hospital. I was so thankful for the third doctor, who administered the shots in the correct place this time, about a month after my hospital stay. This certainly was not a life or death situation, but a lot of intense pain could have been avoided by a correct diagnosis by the first doctor, instead of a guess that my problem was bursitis.

In medicine, and in all aspects of life, it is usually important to be correct, especially if someone's life depends on it. I suggest that you make sure you and your doctor read the X-ray plates together. Don't accept the radiologist's reading alone, especially if it involves a very serious matter.

"Physicians of all men are most happy.
What good success they do have, the world proclaimeth,
and what faults they do commit, the earth covereth."

—Francis Quarrels

The Burn Botch

While visiting my family doctor to get a refill on my usual prescription, I happened to show him a burn I had on my shin. I was too embarrassed to say how I burned my leg, and I didn't tell him. I had been to a dermatologist several times and I had observed how they used liquid nitrogen to freeze or remove common actinic keratosis, better known as pre-cancerous cells. Able to recognize these spots, I felt that maybe, hopefully, just maybe, I could remove it myself using dry ice.

As the saying goes, "I am my own worst enemy."

Before you judge me, please know that I had successfully removed many skin tags and moles by using natural methods such as applying apricot kernel oil, or vitamin E, or even the old sulfur match and copper penny tricks we used for years to get rid of warts. I remembered a doctor telling me years ago that he could remove my son's birthmark with dry ice, so I thought, Why not? I'll give it a try.

I was actually able to remove a few spots, but the one on my shin wasn't progressing the way I thought it should. Clearly, in retrospect, I wasn't knowledgeable enough to treat it like a burn. Right here and now, I must warn you: Don't try the dry ice method.

The doctor examined it, and even though it was a little red around the burn, he thought it looked like it was healing nicely. (Of course I did not tell him the burn was self-inflicted.)

He explained, "There isn't much circulation on the shin bone, therefore things do not heal very quickly in that area."

Soon after, my sister and I left on a trip to visit her daughter. During the trip, the area on my shin became unusually red and swollen. I wrapped it in a wet towel and kept it elevated as much as possible until I returned to the doctor's office 10 days later.

This time, the doctor sent me straight to the hospital where diagnostic tests were performed. When the report came from the laboratory, it revealed that there was a bacterial infection in the wound. The only answer was a strong antibiotic to be administered by IV for two weeks. All the usual admittance tests, including the chest X-rays and blood work, were performed. I couldn't believe I was being admitted to the hospital just for a little burn about the size of a silver dollar.

Fortunately, I remembered the advice of my neighbor: Drink buttermilk or eat yogurt while taking an antibiotic for any length of time. Her husband had injured his shin bone and he'd been required to take antibiotics for a long time, too. Unfortunately, he hadn't known about yogurt then and he had suffered more with a yeast infection.

Antibiotics can destroy good, as well as bad, bacteria. Buttermilk or yogurt helps to replace the body's normal flora, which builds up natural antibodies to ward off a yeast infection. My doctor did not recommend it, so I made a special request for a little carton of buttermilk with my meal tray every day. When I first started to drink it, it tasted so bad I thought I'd rather chance the yeast infection! But eventually I began to like it. The results were enough—I never developed the uncomfortable condition.

The nurses always wondered why I was so interested in my IV hook up. I told them about a friend who had come out of the hospital with her arm swollen to double its size. The needle had been incorrectly inserted when she was unconscious, and there was no one there to notice how her arm had reacted. It took about a week for the swelling to go down. I was determined that the same thing would not happen to me.

All of the nurses checked my ID bracelet before changing my medicine. Even though they had become well-acquainted with me, I still wanted to make sure the right medicine was in that little plastic bag. More than one case of mistakenly giving one patient's medicine to another patient has certainly occurred.

I have a very good friend with Crohn's disease who must spend time in the hospital frequently to receive the nourishment necessary for her well-being. On one occasion, a wrong dose of medicine was given to her intravenously. She'd been conscious at the time, and knew the effect she was feeling was strange, scary, and far from normal. But sometimes waiting for the nurse to answer the call button takes quite a while. At some point, she simply dragged her IV stand to the doorway and shouted for help. The nurse was apparently thankful that my friend did not report her. After that, all of the nurses were very careful with her treatment.

There was no pain in my leg during my stay. It wasn't necessary for me to be confined to bed, except while the bags of medicine dripped slowly into my vein. I had bathroom privileges, and could even take advantage of bathing in that huge bathtub. Of course, I kept my one leg drooped over the side of the tub to avoid getting the bandage wet. Not too many patients were given permission to experience the luxury of this grand tub. This time I had brought my own laxatives, vitamins, and sleeping pills, and I kept them hidden from the nurses. I felt so smug—I could take my sleeping pills when and if I needed one.

It was a fairly comfortable stay; I even joked about it being like the Ritz Carlton. Don't get me wrong, the hospital is never like going to a hotel, even though you're paying 10 times more. And you never have a choice about the room itself. If the view out the window is a brick wall, you're stuck with it. No choice of view, roommate, or bathroom, and no chance to try the mattress!

During this particular stay, my bed was hard and uncomfortable. I wonder if there is one special company that manufactures mattresses for hospitals? What material do they use to make them so hard? Cement? Rocks? When my visitors came, they expected me to lie in that hard bed while they enjoyed the relative comfort of the room's two chairs.

When you are in the hospital for two weeks, you usually have a variety of patients in Bed B. I had one roommate who insisted on parading around our room, not caring one bit if that show-all hospital gown was showing all or not. I wondered how she could stare so long at the chart the nurses instructed her to mark after voiding. First, voiding had to be explained to her. She was very attractive and lots of fun, and I enjoyed her in spite of her immodesty.

One evening while my husband was visiting me, I watched his eyes nearly pop out of his head. My roommate came out of the bathroom, stood at the lavatory with her back to us while she washed her hands, with her cute little derriere completely exposed.

I said to my husband, "Don't look!" But that was just like serving the family a delicious meal and telling them not to eat.

On one occasion, a sedated patient in Bed B wasn't quite *with it* when she started yelling, "Help me get these d— pickles off the shelf!"

I was startled out of a very relaxed state, almost asleep after a surgery, but I had the presence of mind to appease her. Calmly, I replied, "I'll help you get the pickles."

Even the other patients won't let you sleep in the hospital.

Although most of my roommates were very pleasant and agreeable, there was one who wanted to dominate the TV. She watched every soap opera on, and there were a lot of them. I've always been determined not to get hooked on soaps. Because daytime TV doesn't interest me, I didn't care, but I am hooked on baseball and the World Series was on that week. I missed Game One while she watched all those silly, senseless sitcoms. The next night, I explained to her emphatically, "Listen, you've had that remote in your hand for three days, and you've had your choice of programs. Tonight, we are going to watch the baseball game!"

She didn't answer me, but I could tell she was miffed. She glared at me like I had taken her favorite toy and flushed it down the toilet. Then she gave the dividing curtain a swift yank, and drew it clear around her bed.

Her doctor possessed a most caring bedside manner, and he noticed from her chart that her blood pressure had risen. He asked her, "Is there something troubling you?"

I could hear her whisper loudly enough for me to hear, "That old lady in the other bed took control of the remote last night and the only thing she watched was the ball game."

Well, she didn't get to first base with that doctor because he had watched the game, too. She neglected to mention that she had controlled the TV watching for the previous three days. So she stewed all night and got her blood pressure up. You know what? I didn't even care. I just thought to myself, it's time to grow up.

Of the many times that I have been in the hospital, she was the only patient in Bed B with whom I had any kind of disagreement. Maybe she was suffering with something that I did not understand, or maybe she just wasn't living in my world. I'm sure she was glad when I was discharged.

"Everyone here brings happiness
Some by coming, some by... going."

So, after a somewhat uneventful two-week stay in the hospital, and after about three weeks of extra care at home (and who knows what the total cost of the medical bills were), there is just a scar about the size of a quarter on my leg. I still believe in home remedies, but I do think I will avoid dry ice and stick to the kind of ice I put in my tea.

I will leave all my keratosis to my very wealthy dermatologist in Florida.

The Blood Clot

Have you ever tried to push an IV stand through the armhole of your nightie? That's the predicament I found myself in after a sponge bath during one of my hospital stays. How did I happen to land up in the hospital this time? Good question.

Two weeks of family company can be pretty exhausting. In order to relax one afternoon after everyone had left, I curled up in an easy chair with an intriguing book, *The Brilliant Idiot*. It was a story about a very intelligent man who suffered from dyslexia, among other learning disorders. It was engrossing, albeit somewhat depressing, but I read on and on, thinking all the while that some turn of events would eventually improve the poor man's life.

While I sat for hours in the same position, I didn't notice that my leg was hurting behind the knee. Will the real idiot please stand up? That is, if she can? When I stood up and walked around, my leg began to swell. I thought exercising it would help, but the more I walked around, the more it hurt.

I remembered what my first doctor used to say, "Let pain be your guide."

I reasoned then that if I didn't walk around too much, it would get better. But you can only sit and lie around for so long. My family watched me limp around for about three days, and then they all chimed in, "Mother, you better get to the doctor!"

I did. My family doctor sent me to the hospital immediately where a specialist performed a diagnostic test using ultrasound to check the blood flow. It revealed a blood clot. When my doctor was notified of the test results, his instructions were to admit me immediately. I begged for a couple of hours so I could complete some errands and pay my health insurance premium that was overdue. I promised the staff I'd be right back.

When I returned to the hospital, I was assigned to a bed where I remained for three days, hooked up to an IV that was supposed to melt the blood clot. It wasn't the IV that would melt the clot, but the stuff in it called Heparin, known as a blood thinner. I learned that blood clots can easily travel through the body to the heart or another vital organ, and can be quite dangerous—sometimes fatal—so I considered myself lucky to get treatment in time. I was also lucky to get a mattress with no rocks in it because I did not leave my bed for three days.

The nurses brought in and connected a KPad, which is the term used for a moist heating pad. While lying down with my leg on that nice warm heating pad, there was no pain at all. I decided that I would enjoy this hospital stay as much as possible.

I called my family at three o'clock in the afternoon to tell them what I thought was good news. It was only a blood clot that had caused the swelling in my leg; I was very comfortable, and would everyone please come and visit me? I certainly did not consider myself in any danger. I wasn't drugged, and nothing gory like an operation was going to happen, so I figured this time of rest should be enjoyed to the max. To my delight, they all came, bringing my requested nightie and toothbrush.

At 11:00 p.m., a nurse came into my room to take my temperature and blood pressure. I believe they refer to this simple task as taking your vital signs, shortened to *vitals*. When the nurse finished her routine, I thought, Now, sweet dreams. Was I crazy? Had I forgotten where I was? At 12:30 a.m., a nurse on the night shift awakened me from a sound sleep to take my vitals again. Now that *ain't* fair. I was too sleepy to resist, complain, or become agitated, but after she left, I could not get back to sleep.

Then, at 3:00 a.m., my light was turned on again. The nurse carefully checked my wrist ID, and replaced the bag that was connected to my IV. I moaned and complained a little about being awakened again, but she sweetly said, "Just try to go back to sleep."

I tried. Finally, I dozed off, only to be awakened again at 6:00 a.m. by a thermometer being stuck in my ear. This time, my complaint was a little more vocal. Even though the nurse was sympathetic, her instructions from the doctor were on my chart and it was her duty to carry them out. I covered my face with a sheet until 7:30 a.m., and this time the doctor had the privilege of waking me. I told him about my rotten night's sleep and asked if it was necessary to be awakened so often.

"No problem," he said, "I will strike the vitals off the chart during the night, and if you would like, I'll order you a sleeping tablet. Then you will be able to go back to sleep easily after they change the IV at 3:00 p.m."

Now, wasn't that simple? All I had to do was ask the doctor.

I rolled over thinking, what a nice doctor I have, and I went soundly to sleep for a whole uninterrupted 20 minutes. At 8:00 a.m., my breakfast tray was delivered with a cheery, "Good morning!"

I opened my eyes to find a friendly nurse serving me a complete breakfast. I thanked her and promptly reminded myself that I was going to enjoy this time of being waited on. I really don't mind hospital breakfasts. After all, how much damage can you do to a bowl of cream of wheat? Besides, the coffee smelled good, the sun was shining through the window, and my heart was full of thanks and praise as I enjoyed being served a good breakfast.

When the nurse picked up my breakfast tray, I asked, "Am I allowed to take a shower?"

I thought it was a reasonable request, but she looked at me as if I'd asked the most absurd question and then she pointed to the needle on the top of my hand. I knew from that look, she wasn't about to unhook me. I had never been hooked up to an IV before and I assumed it could easily be made more portable.

"You are not allowed to take a shower," she said. "You are allowed to take a sponge bath," she added in a condescending voice. "Get up and I'll show you how easily this stand rolls. You can use the sink in the bathroom, and then I want you to hop right back into bed again. The doctor's orders are to keep you off your feet."

I was very thankful for the bathroom privileges! At least there would be no bedpan for me. The nurse showed me the towels and clean hospital gowns. After bathing, I cheerfully brought out my own nightie, thinking all the while how soft it would feel against my skin.

I pulled my nightie over my head, put my right arm through, and realized I was in big trouble. There was no way I'd be able to pull that IV contraption through the sleeve of my nightie. Obviously, hospital gowns were designed with the IV stand in mind. I had no choice but to put my pretty nightie back into my bag and reluctantly don the institutional gown.

Hospitalitis—what I call a state of existing contentment—set in very quickly. I ordered the works for lunch, and even requested a nice, large red apple for a 4:00 p.m. snack. My sister came to visit with a Scrabble game and wished that she could trade places with me. I was obviously enjoying my time so much, that my visitors were becoming envious!

That afternoon, one of the Sisters came in and told us the cutest joke:

> *"Three mice died and went to heaven. St. Peter wanted to make sure they were happy, and asked if there was anything he could do for them. The mice were very happy, but complained that heaven was such an expanse of beauty, and they were not able to get around to see the wonder of it all. St. Peter fitted each of them with a pair of roller skates, and they left happily.*
>
> *Then, a cat died and went to heaven. After the cat was there for about a week, St. Peter asked the cat how she liked it there. The cat replied, 'This place is unbelievable! Those meals on wheels are delicious!'"*

On the third day, the doctor was very pleased that all of the swelling had gone from my leg and he told me he would release me from the hospital the next morning. My husband and I waited impatiently. We had plans to visit friends in Boone, North Carolina, that weekend. My leg looked and felt fine, and we were hoping it would be okay for me to travel the eight hours in the car to get there. The doctor usually came in to visit much earlier, but he did not come to my room until almost 11:00 a.m. on this particular day.

He gave me a prescription for Coumadin, to keep the blood thinned, and told us that it would be all right for me to travel, as long as I went to a hospital in North Carolina for a blood test upon arrival. He impressed upon me the importance of taking the Coumadin, and also, more importantly, to have it carefully monitored. We agreed to obey his orders.

I felt good traveling because I was so thoroughly rested. The trip seemed to be going very quickly until we decided to stop at a McDonald's for drinks. I ordered a milk shake, a cup of coffee, and a glass of water. We drove happily down the road for 45 miles when I noticed my purse was not at my side where I usually keep it. Now I don't know how your husband would react to such an announcement, but I really wasn't too surprised at my husband's answer.

He asked in disgust, "Well, where did you leave it hanging this time?"

I reluctantly told him, "I think it's in the restroom at McDonald's."

He shook his head in disbelief, "Did you lay it down while you washed your hands and forget to pick it up?"

"No. I hung it over the paper holder in the stall."

Then, there was the all-important question: "How much money did you have in there?"

"I had a $100 in the zippered pocket," I answered nonchalantly. To be honest, I wasn't too concerned about the money. I was more concerned about the Coumadin that was in the purse.

We pulled off at the next highway plaza where we saw another McDonald's. The manager called the other branch 20 miles back, who then relayed the message to the first restaurant and learned that, yes, the manager there had the purse. My husband was relieved and he suggested we pick up the purse on the way home.

"We can't," I had to confess. "I need it now because my Coumadin is in it."

I was so happy and relieved when my purse was found. My driver's license, credit cards, medical cards, all the ID needed for someone to steal my identity were in there, too. Even my library card.

When I mentioned that one to my husband, he moaned, "What in the world are you worrying about your library card for?"

Then the grumbling went into second gear. I really couldn't blame him for feeling that way because I felt badly myself for being so careless. After we traveled the 90 miles to get back to where we started, we realized how late it was. We called our friends and they recommended we get a motel somewhere in the area because their place in the mountains was hard to find, even in the daylight.

No Vacancy signs were displayed at every major hotel. We were weary and disappointed as we traveled on, looking for any vacancy sign. Finally, we found one. It was a small motel that was completely filled except for one room. My husband went to the office to talk with the desk clerk and soon returned to get my opinion.

"They only have one room left. The air conditioner is broken and the room stinks," he reported.

"Good. We'll take it," was my response.

Though he was surprised by my answer, I think he was glad, too. We were both so tired.

Leaving the door open to allow some fresh air in, we discovered the lavatory was spotless and the sheets were clean. We stretched out in bed and were soon sound asleep. I can honestly say, it was one of the best nights of sleep I've ever had in a motel.

We enjoyed our visit with our friends and, yes, we found a local hospital for the blood testing. The nurse there reemphasized the importance of monitoring this particular blood thinner. She said it could cause a stroke if there was bleeding in the brain. She also examined my leg to make sure there was no evidence of a blood clot and kindly reminded me to follow the doctor's instructions to take the drug for exactly the amount of time he'd prescribed.

Since that blood clot, I try to make sure I am in a comfortable position if I am reading for any length of time. I also remind myself to keep my purse by my side and never leave it in a restroom!

A Medical Miracle

"Give credit where credit is due and praise to whom praise belongs."

I do believe that faith and a strong desire to live are important factors in many successful surgeries. When my sister visited a cardiologist about four years ago, she was sent home without much hope. There was a blood clot lodged in her heart, in addition to a leaking valve. She was overdue for a second surgery on another valve that had been damaged by rheumatic fever and repaired 15 years earlier.

Needless to say, she had been forced to live a very limited lifestyle. She avoided all conflict and emotional stress, not to mention physical activity. She did enjoy watching baseball games, but had to leave the room when the games became too exciting. There wasn't much life left without the ball games, as far as she was concerned, but, somehow, she lived. A whole year passed before she returned to the clinic for another evaluation and consequent heart surgery. That year of life was only part of her miracle, though.

It also was, as she said, the longest year of her life. She bought a cemetery plot and paid an extra hefty amount to place the vault in the ground, and she invested money for her funeral. She never thought once of buying new clothes.

I am sure that she entertained thoughts of death many times during this period, even though she did not express them to me, and gave little indication as to how she really felt. Faith, hope, trust, and her determined attitude were so important in her case, in fact vital to her life and the treatment she expected to receive.

Her doctor at the clinic really did not expect to see her again. This was one time he was glad he was wrong, because he really liked my sister. It was her quiet, gentle spirit that impressed him, as she literally stared death in the face with no fear, but trust.

As we waited at her bedside the evening before her operation, two handsome, young, enthusiastic doctors who were part of the operating team came bounding into her room, leaving her with the impression that they were more than ready to accept this challenge. Yes, give praise and credit where it is due, so I will laud the praises of these young surgeons. They certainly encouraged us as they spoke with no fear of failure. These heart surgeons' daring attitude revealed that they seemed to thrive on the impossible.

My sister wasn't given much of a choice. Either she submitted to the surgery or she would most likely die. Until being faced with a decision like that, I don't think anyone can really understand how she felt as she waited to be taken to the operating room the next morning.

Her transporter that day knew the anxiety surgery patients face. He tried to keep the conversation light and keep her mind on something positive. He bantered with her husband about baseball, then directed his last remark to her, "Don't you worry, honey. I haven't lost one yet. I'll be back for you."

Those few words greatly encouraged her husband while he sat in the waiting room for those long hours.

And they did it! The seven hour, very delicate open-heart surgery was successful. They removed the blood clot, repaired one valve, and inserted a mechanical valve. We were all so relieved. It was over! She remained on a monitor in intensive care for about two or three days before being placed in a room. All seemed to be well. Her husband stayed with her every minute.

Late one afternoon, when his wife looked distressed, he ran screaming into the hall for help. I don't know what he saw that alarmed him, and my sister has no remembrance at all of being quickly transported into the operating room for the second time. She was forced to suffer through another surgery. Quickly, that same team of doctors arrived, prepared to do the surgery again. They found a ruptured blood vessel and repaired it. After the second surgery, she was monitored for a longer time, with the very real possibility that she would not survive another invasion of her body. When her condition was clearly stable, she was moved to a room.

How can you get out of the hospital alive? In this case, it was a caring husband who was determined to stay with his wife to make sure everything would be all right. Nurses can only do so much. Doctors, nurses, patients themselves, and even the family can play a vital roll in recovery and healing. If her husband had not been in the room with her, she surely would have died.

The first time I visited my sister after both surgeries, I entered, then backed out of the room before she saw me so that I could compose myself. Her entire arm was black and blue, the rest of her complexion was yellow, and to be honest, my first thoughts were not of faith. Maybe those doctors weren't right after all, I thought for a moment. But after a week, she was almost able to go home.

She simply looked at her black and blue arm and said, "Oh, the nurse said the dark color will go away in a few days."

On one occasion, when her husband left me to care for her, she motioned for me to come very near. I leaned over to hear her whisper very softly, "I'd like to have some potato chips."

Are you crazy? Potato chips? I wanted to blurt out. Of course, I didn't. Instead, I promised, "I'll see if I can find a vending machine."

That's all she wanted, potato chips. I felt like reminding her that salty chips are not good for anyone, let alone a heart patient, but I felt sorry for her and reasoned that a small gesture of kindness was just what she needed.

I had promised my brother-in-law that someone would stay with my sister every minute of every day, and just then, a nurse came into the room. I made sure she would be there for 10 minutes, though I doubt if she or anyone else would have approved of the potato chips. I left the room quickly to find that vending machine. I took the elevator down and back up to the seventh floor in an effort to get back to her room as quickly as possible. Waiting impatiently for those heavy doors to *slowly* open and close, I thought I would have an anxiety attack!

I rushed back to her room, where she was expectantly awaiting those potato chips. Then she only ate six of them! That was all she wanted. I went to all that trouble for six chips! I thought she was hungry. I found out later, she just wanted something tasty that she liked. She was fed up with that bland hospital food.

My sister certainly values life today! There is nothing like a close brush with death to make anyone appreciate the light of a new day, the laughter of children and grandchildren, a baseball game, birds singing in the morning, a good night's sleep in your own bed, or a tasty meal of potato chips.

A team of well-trained, daring doctors, combined with the faith of a patient and the loving care of a husband, equaled a medical miracle.

The Head Injury

The children living in my son's neighborhood would usually gather to play in his fenced backyard. The sounds of laughter and occasional arguing let their folks know that they were all safe. They were not supervised every minute and, unfortunately, sometimes that's all it takes for someone to get hurt. Unbeknownst to his parents, one of the neighborhood kids brought his father's golf club with him one day and was swinging it around wildly.

I am sure that the blow to my grandson's head was not intentional. As a two-and-a-half-year-old child, he did not realize the danger he was in when he walked blithely behind the boy with the swinging club. In truth, a golf club can be a lethal weapon.

On that day, the happy, playful sounds ceased as he collapsed, screaming in pain. His dad realized immediately how serious the head injury could be. The club had struck him right in the middle of the back of his head. He was rushed to the hospital just blocks away and treated in the emergency room.

After some medication was administered, my grandson began to convulse. More medication was given, which caused him to hallucinate. The medicine seemed only to complicate the problem.

My son stayed with his little boy until midnight. By then, the drugs had worn off a bit. His tongue was no longer protruding from his lips in an abnormal fashion, and that alone relieved him. Just after midnight, the boy fell into a sound sleep. Assuming he would sleep right through the night, my son returned home to get his own much needed rest.

He returned to the hospital at 6:30 the next morning to check on his son. The bed in his room was empty and his first thought was that the very worst had occurred. He tore down the hall to the nurses' station to learn what had happened. The nurse directed him to the X-ray department, which was in the basement of the large hospital. As soon as the elevator doors opened, he could hear his son screaming. At first, he was glad to hear those screams. But then, as he entered an X-ray room, he found two technicians with their feet propped up on a table, waiting for his son to finish his temper tantrum so they could take his X-rays.

My son was livid—too angry to even speak. He burst into the darkened room and found his son lying on a cold X-ray table, screaming about bugs that he thought were crawling all over him. Here was this small child, suffering from hallucinations, having been awakened by strangers at 6:00 a.m. and rolled to an X-ray room on a gurney, placed on a cold metal table, and he was expected to lie still so that he could be X-rayed. He surely didn't even know what an X-ray was.

My grandson probably felt like he'd been rescued from some sort of hell when his daddy picked him up with his big, strong arms and held him close for a long time. From then on, he wanted to be sure that his daddy was right beside him while the X-rays were taken.

At my son's request, he was released soon after the X-rays were completed. He decided he could give the boy better care and attention at home. The drugs wore off and the hallucinations stopped. Fortunately, the skull had not been fractured and there was no permanent damage to his head or to his brain.

This is just another example of why many parents will go without any sleep at all, or sleep in a chair, rather than leave their young children in the hands of the hospital staff. Medical professionals are trained to complete tasks, but not always to care for and comfort patients. By all means, stay with a child who needs you now—more than if he was home in his own bed. Doctors offer treatments, order tests for diagnostic purposes, and administer drugs, but they don't offer much nurturing or love. Parents: It is our responsibility to administer the TLC.

Bacteria in the Hospital

Everything in a hospital appears to be handled in a very clean, hygienic, and sterile manner. Nurses and doctors are always snapping those examining gloves on and off, and used needles are tossed into special containers. For the most part, hands are washed. Operating rooms are ice cold, so that bacteria will not easily grow there. Surgeons don clean gowns and masks, and scrub both themselves and their patients with antiseptics. The rooms seem to be mopped every day, and even those little trash bags that hang on your cart are removed daily, even if there is nothing in them. It is hard to comprehend, then, why so many different infections are contracted in hospitals.

An acquaintance of mine had her knee operated on recently, and wouldn't you know it, she picked up a terrible staph infection. It baffles both patients and hospital administrators when statistics are reported about the multitude of infections that are acquired in hospitals.

One time when I was a patient, I was walking the hospital hall and I met another patient who made a curious observation and wanted me to confirm it. Apparently, the cleaning lady had come into her room, cleaned the lavatory sink, and then, with the same rag, went into the bathroom and cleaned the toilet. Immediately afterward, she entered the next room and cleaned the lavatory with the same rag she had used on the toilet in the former room! My fellow patient asked me to pay attention to what the cleaning lady did in my room next time she came. I was amazed to find that this woman seemed to have only one rag at her disposal. Sure enough, she cleaned my room in the same way.

"If you don't report this, I will," I said to my comrade. She agreed. Either this cleaning person was not following instructions, or she was just plain lazy, or she didn't realize the necessity of cleanliness.

Some hospital workers seem to think that the gloves they wear are intended to protect only themselves. They seem not to realize that germs can live just as well on latex as on skin! I imagine nurses must get tired of washing their hands every time they enter a patient's room, but I think that's what is necessary to keep from spreading germs from one patient to another.

From an article in the *Sun-Sentinel*:

CADAVER TISSUE SUSPECTED IN
KNEE-OPERATION DEATH

State health officials found no link between the deaths of three men who had undergone elective knee surgeries last month. The youngest patient, a 23 year-old man, was infected with the clostridium sordelli bacterium, state health officials said Thursday.

The bacterium is suspected to have come from a cadaver's tissue that was grafted into the patient," said Dr. Harry Hull, the state epidemiologist. He said clostridium sordellii grows naturally in corpses as part of the decomposition process. He didn't know why two other men, ages 78 and 60, died after their knee surgeries in the same hospital.

Most hospital-acquired infections, or mistakes in medicine, are overlooked and forgotten by most of the millions of patients who, with grateful hearts, leave the hospital in better health than when they entered. Most of the hospital staff are highly trained and they carefully maintain the sterility that is absolutely necessary to protect patients in the hospital environment. While there is room for improvement in the care given patients by hospital employees, it will only happen when diligence is practiced by the patients themselves and when patients begin to hold hospitals and their staff accountable for their actions.

The Alternate Route to the Hospital

My daughter, who is a school teacher, has a friend named Sandy who is the school's guidance counselor. Sandy is also the undefeated golf pro in her league and she is a vivacious, young looking, 55-year-old woman.

While driving her SUV alone on an open highway one day, she noticed a red car suddenly cross the center divider of the road and head directly toward her.

"Come on, baby, move it over," was her last thought as she noticed that the driver, a young blonde woman, was talking on a cell phone and focusing her attention on something on the passenger side seat.

When she realized that this driver was not going to yield in time to avoid hitting her, she quickly swerved her SUV into a rough, steep ditch. The vehicle fishtailed and slid along on its side into the ditch, where all the windows broke, glass flying everywhere. The sound of crumpling metal was deafening. She felt certain these were the last seconds of her life.

She doesn't remember exactly what happened next, but somehow, the SUV must have hit something in the ditch that set the sliding vehicle upright. Finally, and unbelievably, the vehicle landed on its wheels, back on the highway.

She felt her hand, and then her shoulder, and then uttered in disbelief, "I'm alive!"

Did Sandy have her seat belt fastened? No! It was a miracle she'd survived. The blonde in the red car quickly sped away and never returned to help.

A woman, who had been traveling directly behind the red car, immediately phoned the police on her cell phone, and then ran to see what she could do to help. Sandy was still sitting helplessly in her SUV. The vehicle was completely smashed and destined for the scrapyard. The helpful woman expected Sandy to be in much worse condition, considering the wreckage.

Blood was running down Sandy's arm, so the woman had no choice but to use the only article of clothing readily available to stop the bleeding.

"Oh, no, not *that* jacket!" Sandy protested.

"I've gotta use it to stop the bleeding," was the excited woman's reply.

Sandy watched as the woman fashioned a tourniquet for her and explained that the now ruined classy jacket had been a gift from the golf team she coached. The woman apologized about the jacket and then went on to thank Sandy for not swerving toward the center of the road, thereby avoiding a head-on collision with her.

When the police arrived, the good Samaritan and witness was able to give a clear and accurate account of the accident. Her testimony cleared Sandy of all responsibility. The emergency squad arrived in record time and they knew exactly what to do. Sandy was impressed by the good-looking paramedics. They looked so young!

"What's your age, ma'am?" was their first question.

Sandy thought to herself, well, now, is that really important? When she didn't respond, she was asked a second time. Now, she thought, why can't they just ask the date of birth and then they can figure it out for themselves? A lot of other information was being recorded at the same time, and when Sandy was asked the third time, she finally mumbled quietly, "55."

The paramedics apparently weren't able to hear her and they thought it best to just move on. Her hurt pride didn't compare with the pain she was feeling in her body, though. She was gingerly placed on a stretcher, and was rushed to the emergency room of a local hospital.

In order to determine the extent of her injuries, the doctor ordered a CAT scan. He suspected a punctured lung and no one had to tell her that her ribs were broken. The paramedics told her that she had also broken either her collar bone or clavicle. The emergency room nurse placed a large collar around her neck for support and to restrain motion.

Badly bruised and bloody, Sandy was forced to drink that awful pink, chalky stuff that is necessary before a CAT scan can be performed. She was transferred from the padded gurney to the hard surface, and for a moment, she thought maybe she would be better off dead because that simple move caused her so much pain. The thought itself died quickly. She knew she wasn't ready. After she was given something for the pain, her only thoughts were of getting better.

Having passed out briefly, she eventually found herself in a hospital bed with the collar on her neck and a soaked gown. That nasty pink stuff hadn't stayed down and she had vomited all over herself.

A nurse removed the gown, helped Sandy into a clean one, and was about to leave when a friend of Sandy's rushed into the room. When this friend had learned of the accident, she had imagined her best friend half-dead and had sped to the hospital to see for herself the extent of her injuries.

The first thing she did was stop the nurse from leaving. She demanded, "You're not leaving here until this dirty collar is replaced with a clean one!"

Sandy said later that she was most grateful for this intervention from her friend. There she was, miserable and lying in bed with a wet, stinking collar right under her nose, but she'd felt powerless to do anything about it. Her friend carefully removed more glass from her hair and wiped off some of the dried blood from her many scratches.

Do we need a friend or family member to watch over us, speak up for us, and even pamper us a little? Oh, yes! Just ask anyone who has endured a CAT scan revealing five broken ribs and a broken clavicle, and has just arrived to the hospital via the emergency room.

Broken ribs heal all by themselves, but oh, the torture you go through in that six weeks of healing time. It hurts to breathe deeply or to cough, and getting out of bed is excruciatingly painful. But ribs do heal.

*

Sandy didn't know who had cut her panties off. She felt naked without them. When her two young sons visited her, she had one request.

"Go home and bring me some underpants. You'll find them in the second drawer on the left in my dresser."

"Awww, Mom," they complained, still embarrassed adolescents.

They quickly returned with her girdle, which she declared would take six arms to pull up. Anyone who has suffered a broken rib, or watched someone else try to tug a girdle up, knows how painful it would be to even try. She had five broken ribs and a broken collar bone, to boot. The boys were sent home a second time to fetch the underpants.

At this point, Sandy wasn't too concerned about whether she would compete in golf again. She thought it best to quit while unbeaten. But she knew she might change her mind when all the aches and pains stopped. And, of course, they did stop, although it took a lot of patience. The body does a wonderful job of repairing itself when given time.

Sandy is very thankful for four things:

1. She had no head injuries.
2. There had been no passengers in her SUV.
3. A helpful passerby witnessed the accident.
4. A friend was there to help her when she needed it.

Will she use her seatbelt now? Need we ask? We must all buckle up our *Sandybelts*, as we now call them.

Saved by a Seatbelt

Two friends of mine, Alice and Bill, were making their first drive to California. At 10:30 in the morning, Alice became so drowsy she could barely stay awake. Her husband was asleep in the passenger seat beside her, so rather than wake him, she kept on driving.

It is a terrible mistake to keep driving when drowsiness hits. The monotony of the long, uneventful drive soon put Alice to sleep, too. It doesn't take too much imagination to guess what happens when the only two people in a car going 70 miles an hour are both asleep.

The car rolled over twice in an open field, strewing all their belongings out of the car's trunk. When the car finally came to a resting position, they were able to unbuckle their seat belts and climb out the windows. A passerby phoned for help and the emergency vehicles arrived quickly to the scene of the self-inflicted accident. The paramedics were amazed by their lack of injuries.

The duty-bound paramedics insisted that Alice lie on the stretcher to be transported to the hospital. One of the first things they attempted was to cut off the sleeve of her jacket so that they could take her blood pressure.

She stopped them by saying, "Wait a minute! This is my favorite jacket. I'll remove it for you."

She easily removed the jacket and complied with their request to be taken to the hospital on the stretcher. Riding in the vehicle's seat is what she would have preferred, but they insisted upon an ambulance ride.

She didn't see her husband until the next day in the hospital. She laughed when she saw him walking down the hall with one of the sleeves cut off his jacket. Amid most tragedies, some small bit of humor can be found. Even though the car had been demolished, plans had been changed, and there were great inconveniences, my friend laughed when she related the story to me. She couldn't help but giggle when she thought of Bill's bare arm hanging out of his jacket.

Medical Misunderstandings

A Friend's Foot Fiasco

You've heard the saying: "When your feet hurt, you hurt all over."

My friend was not a complainer. I had always wondered why she shifted her weight from one foot to the other whenever we stood visiting. Now I know the reason. Her feet were killing her.

My friend suffered with arthritic feet for a number of years until the constant pain finally compelled her to seek the help of a surgeon. The doctor won her confidence and she trusted him when he said it would be a simple, two-hour operation.

Instead, she endured a four-hour operation, during which the doctor felt it was necessary to take bone from her hip. It left her with a deep, eight-inch incision. Metal was fused to the bone in her foot, and then a plaster cast was applied. The dictates of the Medicare program do not allow hospitalization for a foot surgery; instead, it is completed on an outpatient basis. So, just hours after her surgery, my friend was on her way home. She assumed the surgery had been a success.

The trip home was quite a painful struggle. She was not prepared with a wheelchair or walker. The pain in her hip was so intense it caused her to vomit the drugs given to her in the hospital, right on the front lawn. Her hip had been agitated by the car ride and her foot was throbbing with pain as well. Her husband gladly performed the duties of a nurse. He tried to comfort his wife and then he raced to the pharmacy to fill the prescribed drug for pain, which was Vicodin.

The doctor had promised my friend that she would be walking in three weeks' time. He never advised her, however, that she would need a wheelchair and a ramp to get around. With the hope that this was only a temporary condition, she was thankful she had such tender loving care given to her by her hubby. Her hip began to heal normally. Her doctor told her she would need therapy for her foot and she looked forward to her scheduled physical therapy sessions.

After her first visit with the therapist, though, she was very disappointed. Her foot was red, swollen, and even more painful. This was not what she had expected at all. Now she was to wear a different type of cast and she was instructed to go home and walk as much as possible.

During repeated visits to therapy, she was given hot and cold baths, ultrasound was used, and she was instructed to ride the exercise bike. The therapist emphasized how important it was for her to walk at home as much as possible.

Her surgery had taken place on May 7th. After three months of therapy and four casts, her foot was not healing correctly. It was still so painful, she couldn't walk on it.

Her therapist continually reminded her in a very stern fashion to walk whenever she could. Her obvious question was, "How can you walk on a foot that is so red and swollen?" She knew that any walking she did only aggravated her foot.

Her husband discussed the situation with a woman who was in charge of the damage control department in the hospital. She implied that his wife was old and senile. He became quite angry. He knew better. He had watched his wife dutifully suffer through another month of therapy, and when she'd sprained her ankle badly when her boot-like cast slipped off the exercise bike pedal, he'd become furious.

He decided to take things into his own hands and do a little investigating. He discovered that all of the therapy centers in the area were owned by the hospital, except for one. He made an appointment with a therapist at this independently owned facility and was amazed when the therapist showed him the manual concerning ultrasound. It emphasized the fact that ultrasound should never be used when metal has been fused to the bone. He even brought his camera into their therapy room and documented how the boots were *strapped* onto the bicycle pedals. Later, he took a snapshot of his wife's boot, the one that had never been strapped down during her therapy bike riding.

When he confronted the hospital authorities with his evidence, his wife suddenly went from old and senile to worthy of the best of care. The hospital treated them in an entirely different fashion.

I can't find anything humorous in this most unfortunate experience, except for the hospital's offer to reimburse them for the gas they would use to visit the alternate therapy center. And, of course, there was their second *kind* gesture to pay for the ice recommended by the second therapist to reduce the swelling and pain.

What was supposed to be a three-week recovery turned into four painfully endured months. After just one week of the correct therapy, my friend's foot improved greatly. To her delight, she could actually begin taking a few steps without pain.

How much was the settlement? Their lawyer advised them to take the hospital's offer of less than $10,000, and "run with it." Maybe you or I would have looked for another lawyer, but they were not greedy. They were just elated and thankful that, finally, she was able to walk again.

The Gorilla

Our dear friend had gone though a routine test that revealed cancer in his prostate gland. Cancer is so indiscriminate. It afflicts our families, our loved ones, young and old, and in this case, our very best friend.

He was known for his humor and fun-loving nature. He was also known for having lots of hair on his body, but not too much on his head. Now, here he was, in a hospital bed, awaiting surgery the next morning.

It was late in the evening, after his wife had gone home, when a rather effeminate male nurse entered his room carrying a razor. "I'm going to shave you now," he declared.

When he lifted my friend's gown, he exclaimed, "Good grief, we have a GORILLA!"

Now, our friend was not a *patient* patient, and he became rather anxious while the nurse lathered him up and began to shave in the area near where the surgery would be. He cautioned the nurse, "Just be careful of *Oscar*."

The shaving continued, and he could feel the nicks and cuts. "For crying out loud! Get a new blade for that dumb razor!" he shouted.

The nurse agreed, left the room, and soon returned with a new razor blade. He checked his work and, once again, my friend warned him not to mess around with *Oscar*. Then the nurse proceeded to shave up the abdominal region and began shaving right on to the chest area.

"Hey, where did you get your instructions?" our friend demanded. "Half the hair on my chest is gone. Wait a minute, I want to see what you've done."

With that, he hopped off the bed and looked at his body in the mirror. The nurse had shaved off most of his body hair, clear up to the nipples.

Our friend didn't think all that shaving had been necessary and he angrily asked the nurse, "Do you know what type of surgery I am scheduled for tomorrow?"

"Don't you know?" was the nurse's reply.

"Don't be funny. Of course I know. But I'm asking you."

Finally, the nurse checked his records and confessed, "I'm sorry. It looks like I made a slight mistake. Someone told me you were having colon surgery."

"You jerk," my friend yelled in the heat of his temper, "you're not supposed to go on what someone says! Read the record, because somebody didn't *tell* you right!"

Needless to say, my friend was wide awake when they rolled him to the operating room in the morning—he wanted to make sure that the doctor had his records straight, too.

The surgery was a success, and all that hair on his chest grew back eventually. My friend lived many happy years before the cancer returned. This time it was in his spine. He was treated with a chemo pill, which he took once a month, and he lived three more active years. With the faith he had, I'm positive somewhere in eternity he is at peace and taking his rest. Knowing him, he's probably cracking jokes with the angels.

The Mammogram

After a tiny malignant tumor, or *cyst*, was discovered on my sister's breast, she urged me to get a mammogram, too. She had decided to be examined because a good friend of hers had been diagnosed with cancer. Her friend had told her, "If you want to see your grandchildren, you better have a mammogram." My sister's operation was successful, and after following a treatment of radiation, she recovered completely.

She warned and nagged me until I finally decided to give in and schedule a mammogram for myself. First, I called my doctor, who gave his referral, and then I waited for the appointment at the hospital. I was impressed by the proficiency of the lab technicians. I undressed from the waist up, donned a cape-like gown, and laid my offering on that cold, metal X-ray table. The intense pressure used to squeeze my breasts worried me, but it was all over quickly. Then I was told to wait before dressing. I don't know what the medical profession would do without the word WAIT. Wait, patient, wait!

Thankfully, this time, I did not have to wait long. All kinds of negative thoughts flooded my mind. Maybe I had advanced breast cancer? I momentarily pictured myself in a casket. I even thought about writing my own eulogy. I felt so sad.

The X-rays, however, were clear. I was told to get dressed, not to worry, and that the results would be sent to my doctor.

A week later, I was in the doctor's office when he pointed out a small, perfectly round shaped cyst on the X-ray of my breast. He was not too concerned because of the size and shape.

He reassured me by saying, "Usually, when a cyst is so round, it isn't malignant."

"Is there a way I can know for sure?" I asked with concern.

"Yes, I could do a biopsy," he said casually.

"Good," I agreed, "We'll do that. Then I won't worry."

At the time, I wasn't aware of all that was involved in a biopsy. To me, *biopsy* meant sticking a little needle in, taking out a tiny piece of tissue, and having it examined by a pathologist. A fairly simple procedure, right? Wrong.

When I told my sister about my scheduled appointment for a biopsy, she volunteered to go with me so that she could drive me home. Her biopsy had been performed by the same surgeon. I was still thinking *needle*, and I declined her offer. I guess she decided to simply let me find out for myself—she could have told me that a biopsy is the next best thing to major surgery.

When I showed up at the hospital as an outpatient, it dawned on me that there was going to be a bit more involved than I had expected. I was feeling very apprehensive as I undressed and put on a hospital gown. And then I waited.

I learned that I could order a glass of cranberry juice and some wafers for a snack. I patiently waited some more. Since I hadn't brought anything to read, the nurse pointed out the TV. I decided to order a cup of coffee and I tried to relax. I'm not fond of waiting, but I do like being served! Just about the time I was getting ready to order another glass of juice, a transporter wheeled in a cart. It was for me, and I was told to get on.

Ah, my chariot has arrived, I thought.

Riding on a gurney can be embarrassing. Why couldn't I be allowed to walk to the operating room? I think those carts should be reserved for the unconscious, or for people who really can't walk. I felt so silly, that I used the sheet to cover my face.

Reality hit when they rolled me into that ice cold operating room. I was completely bathed above the waist and I was lathered with some kind of antiseptic. A partial tent-like screen was used to block my vision of the operation. I'm sure a local anesthetic was used, but I don't remember the prick. All this preparation seemed needless for what I thought was a simple procedure.

I felt the surgeon tugging away at my breast and the warm blood trickling down my side and I wondered what was going on. Finally, I had to ask, "Is all this necessary for a biopsy?"

"Dear, this procedure is a called a lumpectomy," he answered gently.

When the surgery was over, the doctor comforted me by saying, "I'm 99 percent sure that the results will confirm my diagnosis. The little round cyst I removed is nothing to worry about."

While I waited for the results, I tried not to worry. I just wanted to be sure. That's why I'd agreed to the biopsy-that-turned-out-to-be-a-lumpectomy in the first place. My older sister had died of lung cancer, my younger sister had just had a malignant cyst removed from her breast, and her good friend had suffered through a mastectomy.

The doctor was right! He called me into his office a week later and used that comforting term, "Benign."

I didn't say anything for a moment after he gave me the news, but the doctor saw the relief and joy in my facial expression. Then, he began to observe me in his knowing way. He had been competent during the procedure, but to inform a patient of such good news overwhelmed even him for a moment. We were not doctor and patient for a moment, just two human beings rejoicing together.

Thank you, doctor!

The Ring Finger?

My friend made an appointment with her family physician regarding a large, unsightly lump on her knuckle. When her doctor examined her middle finger, he called it a tumor and referred her to an orthopedic surgeon.

Orthopedists are specialists and they prefer referrals. I guess it's a lot easier to have another doctor diagnose the problem and supply him with a patient history. Then, I suppose they can get to the root of the problem right away. Orthopedists are also extremely busy doctors. Let's call this orthopedist Doctor O.

There is always a two-week waiting period to get into his office, and then, if you are lucky, you will only wait an hour to see him. Doctor O played golf and so did my friend. The fact that the office waiting room was well-stocked with golf magazines made waiting a little more enjoyable for her. I've always found that the selection of reading material in a doctor's waiting room will give you a good indication of what interests he and/or his wife have.

My friend presented her medical records to the nurse, who placed them in a rack on the door of the consultation room where my friend waited some more.

Doctor O was a no-nonsense doctor. After seeing her finger, he immediately ordered surgery to be scheduled. But first came the laboratory tests consisting of the chest X-ray and blood work. This meant another day of waiting in the hall of the hospital. In the lab hall, there were chairs provided, but no reading material.

As she left, the nurse gave my friend the usual instructions: Nothing by mouth after midnight, bathe, and appear at the hospital by 7:00 a.m.

Her medical records were sent on to the hospital from the orthopedist's office. On the day of the surgery, she returned to the hospital and signed the necessary papers giving consent to operate on her third finger—the one with the very obvious tumor on the knuckle. Then, of course, there was more waiting and preparation.

My friend's husband was told his wife's surgery would probably take two hours. The staff suggested he go for breakfast, which he did gladly. I am sure that any man, if given the choice, would prefer breakfast over waiting around in a hospital waiting room. Not only do patients need patience, but spouses need it, too.

In preparation for the surgery, my friend was anesthetized. Before operating, Doctor O looked carefully at her hand. He didn't even need his glasses to see that the lump to be removed was on what he called *tall man* not on the ring finger. But when my friend had signed the permission papers, she'd noted the third finger, counting from her pinky, or from her thumb. Either way, when *she* looked at her hand, the *tall man* was the third finger. The hospital staff counted from her index finger, excluding her thumb, which is not technically a finger. It was a case of mistaken fingers.

Now what to do? The patient was out cold and consent was needed to operate on the correct finger. The solution? Find the husband to sign the consent! But he had already left the building for breakfast. Doctor O was left with the only alternative: Bring the patient, who had already been anesthetized, back to consciousness.

While my friend was still partially sedated, under the bright lights of the operating room, the surgeon began to explain, "We can't find your husband..."

Immediately thinking the worst, she panicked, not waiting for him to finish. "What do you mean you can't find him? Where is he?"

"You're husband is fine," Doctor O said, trying to comfort her, but she interrupted him again. "But you can't find him!"

"We told him to go for breakfast."

"He went to breakfast without me?" she asked, thoroughly confused.

Doctor O realized it would take another minute or two for his patient to be able to comprehend what he needed her to do. He explained that there had been a mistake. Her ring finger had been identified as the third finger, when in fact, it was her middle finger, or *tall man* that was in need of repair. Before operating, they needed permission in writing to operate on the correct finger. Since her husband had left for breakfast, Doctor O was requesting, "Would you please sign the permission form?"

She signed.

Talk about technicalities! There was no doubt where the tumor was, yet the doctor *had* to have it on paper in black and white. Strange maybe, but this is actually the type of surgeon I would choose—the kind who checks the details and is not likely to make a mistake.

My friend was lucky in that the tumor was so noticeable. Patients must be just as careful and specific as doctors when communicating, so as to prevent medical errors.

Beds, Backs, and Beyond

My Achy Brachy Back

One very important thing I learned as a back patient was from the third doctor I consulted about the problem. He said, without hesitation or consideration for my feelings, "No doctor will ever help you."

Completely devastated in spirit, I did not want to believe him. But in the end, he was right, and I was dead wrong to continue to try and seek help from the orthopedist, pain management clinics, chiropractors, neurosurgeons, medical doctors, doctors of osteopathy and prolotherapy. Many of the recommended treatments actually increased the pain in my back, not to mention the anguish in my mind.

Knowing what I know now, I have come to my own conclusion. The reason the medical professionals can't help heal a back patient is because they just don't know how, nor do they want to bother. Some even suffer with back problems themselves.

I was afflicted with my back problem for a whole year before I saw an orthopedic doctor, and I don't think I would have gone to a doctor at all had I not been urged by a family member to do so. My daughter noticed how I continually switched positions in the car, trying to get comfortable, and said, "Mother, go to the doctor!"

My back problem began as a result of two separate injuries. The first injury occurred while I was sledding at the age of 50. The old saying, "You are as old as you feel," just *ain't* so, at least not when ligaments are involved. I was having such fun, acting like a 5-year-old playing in the snow; I started down the hill, lying on a big coaster sled, my sister ran and flung herself on top of me, and down we flew. When we hit what we called the "soup bowl," she went up, the sled went down, and I got sandwiched in between. I felt something *give* in the middle of my back. Now try to communicate that to a doctor.

The second time, a few months later, I was lifting a heavy object without bending my knees, and I had a more intense feeling in the very same part of my spine. It began to really nag me, especially while sitting or lying down.

The First Orthopedist

The first doctor, an orthopedist, did not spend much time with me on my first visit. He needed some kind of tangible proof to tell him what was wrong, so he ordered X-rays. I knew that it would take at least two weeks to get an appointment. I also knew that it would mean at least an hour of waiting in his office, reading his wife's old magazines. The average wait time in most orthopedists', neurosurgeons', or specialists' offices that I have experienced was between one and two hours. The average amount of time actually spent with the doctor has been three minutes, if that.

When I finally returned with all of my X-rays, and they had been reviewed by the doctor, I was told there was nothing wrong with my back. His solution was to give me a set of exercises. I had never suffered any pain down my leg until I did those exercises. I made another appointment and waited patiently, like a good and ignorant patient, to see that doctor again. After all, the exercises he had told me to do had made my back pain worse. Did he want to help me? No. Instead, he did what many doctors do: He took no responsibility for my condition, but referred me to another doctor.

Because the X-rays hadn't revealed anything wrong with the alignment of my spine, and I was not in obvious excruciating pain, he insisted there was nothing wrong with my back. When I insisted that there definitely was, he became indignant, arrogant, and almost rude. He never took the time to explain what could possibly be my problem, and when I mentioned the pain in my back muscles, he merely dismissed the complaint as a muscle cramp.

I now know that torn ligaments do *not* show up on X-rays. After all of the descriptions I had given him, he simply never bothered to explore the idea of a torn ligament. I learned on my own that muscles take over to help support the spine when there is an injury in one or more ligaments, and when the muscles become tired, they cramp. Unfortunately, it took a long time for me to come upon that knowledge.

The Neurosurgeon

The orthopedic surgeon ended up referring me to a neurosurgeon. He'd caught on by now that I'm an insistent person and he wanted to get me off his back. I'm sure he knew that I did not need the services of a neurosurgeon, or at least he should have known. Why do I have to learn everything the hard way?

I patiently waited four weeks for the appointment with the neurosurgeon, and two more hours in his office. Obviously, neurosurgeons are surgeons and are not too interested in anything other than surgery. He advised me to submit to a myelogram that, once again, revealed that there was nothing wrong with my back. He decided that two weeks of bed rest would be beneficial. It was not. In fact, it further weakened the muscles in my back that were cramping.

He decided that a back brace was necessary. Although my back felt better during the day, wearing the brace continued to weaken my back and it didn't help a bit when I took it off at night. It was strange that my back felt so good during the day, with or without the brace, but when I wanted to lie down in bed, that nagging feeling, like something slipping out of place, was even worse. I tried to envision a way to sleep standing up.

I was relieved when he finally pronounced that no surgery was necessary, although I already knew in my heart that this was true and that I was wasting my time sitting in surgeons' offices. I understand that many back surgeries are successful, but I also know that some of them are not. Our doctor in Florida had told us that he'd been on the gurney, rolling into the operating room, when he'd learned that there was a 50/50 chance of his making a complete recovery. He made a quick decision, hopped off the gurney, and canceled the surgery.

The Second Orthopedist

Over a period of 25 years, I continued to try different doctors and various treatments for my back. I remained active and I felt fairly good during the day. But at night when I lay down to relax, again it felt like something was slipping out of place. It felt like someone's knuckle was pressing into the middle of my back. It would usually take me hours of twisting and tossing around to get comfortable enough to get to sleep. There were some mornings when I felt like I had been run over by a Mack truck.

I learned the hard way that orthopedists and neurosurgeons do not like to give any type of relaxants to a back patient. On the other hand, I have found that general physicians are much more generous with drugs to make us feel more comfortable. We did not have a regular family doctor at that time—our family had been so healthy, we had not thought it necessary. That's hard for me to even imagine today.

I was so disappointed after I visited the second orthopedist who very briefly examined me and said that no doctor would ever be able to help. He sent me out of his office with a prescription for a small amount of Valium. That helped a little, but I never bothered with him again.

Months later, another orthopedist came close to the right treatment when he put me in the hospital for 10 days with a brace strapped onto me. He ordered me to walk the halls for eight hours a day. I followed his orders and walked and walked and walked. I was not allowed to sit, except for the ride in the uncomfortable wheelchair used to take me to therapy. This, of course, did not make any sense to me. I was to walk all day, just not to the therapy room.

It also didn't make sense to me that I was forced to lie down to eat. Eating my meals flat on my back was rather awkward and messy, but I eventually got used to it. If the doctor had not also ordered the intermittent traction treatments, and given me bed rest instead, it might have done some good. It was terribly disappointing to go home, still feeling that nagging pressure right at my waist.

Of course, this doctor said, just like the rest of them, that there was nothing more he could do, and there was nothing more that *should* be done for my back. Once again, I learned the hard way. The doctor was right, and I, the patient, was wrong to keep seeking help from the medical people in white.

Drug Therapy

Naturally, I didn't stop there. Another doctor tried drug therapy with me. I had never taken many drugs and this particular drug hit me like a ton of bricks. I felt like I was walking around on cloud nine during the day, but I still felt that nagging feeling at night before I drifted off into never-never land. By the end of the week, I couldn't remember if I'd taken my pill or not. I'm not sure what the doctor or I expected that pill to do.

When my daughter came home from college, I wanted to take her shopping. I'd forgotten if I'd taken a pill or not, so I took another one. While shopping in a rather upscale store, she sensed I wasn't quite right, so she parked me in a dressing room with our packages while she continued to browse. Pretty soon, she heard a crashing commotion in the dressing room and mumbled to herself, "Oh no, mother fell off the bench."

In fact, it was just the packages that had slipped to the floor. Neither she nor I realized how *high* I was. When I got behind the wheel of the car to drive home, I put the car in drive instead of reverse and lightly bumped the fence. Then I put the car in reverse and hit a car driving into the parking lot. I could have sworn the car hadn't been there. Luckily, there was very little damage and the driver of the car was a nurse who took one look at my eyes and knew I definitely didn't belong behind the wheel. My daughter looked on in horror as I tried to talk my out way out of a ticket with a police officer, occasionally slurring my words. Thankfully, the nurse arranged for us to be taken home.

A week later, when I returned to the doctor who had prescribed the drug, I related this incident to him. The medicine he had given me should either have been administered by someone responsible, someone other than the patient, or at least the physician should have recommended buying one of those pill dispensers to keep me from overdosing on the strong medicine. He did not make another appointment for me and he asked me in a firm tone not to come back. I was only too happy to oblige.

Pain Management Clinic

Sometimes, the problem is in the way we see the problem ourselves. I finally decided that there was no solution to my back injury and I would have to deal with the problem in my own way. Then, someone else would come into my life who would insist that another treatment or doctor could help me. Many, many times, I would wait six weeks for an appointment, only to be disappointed again. Or, I would read an article in the newspaper or a magazine about new treatments for a bad back. I always hated that expression, "bad back."

I wasn't exactly searching for a cure when I followed a referral to visit a pain management clinic. The doctor in charge of the clinic had a back problem similar to mine. You'd think I'd be smart enough to recognize that if this doctor wasn't able to cure his own back problem, he probably would not be able to do much for mine either. I almost canceled, but was glad I kept the appointment. He offered something more than all the others—hope. He also acknowledged that there was something wrong with my back, and was willing to work with me for a cure.

He advised me to keep my body in a pelvic tilt position—which is just what it sounds like—continually. I was to lie on the floor as often as I could during the day to practice the pelvic tilt, and I was to take a drug to relax the muscles when I was not doing the pelvic tilt.

The doctor advised me to take a low dose of Elavil each day for a week, and then increase the dosage weekly until I could take one whole tablet (that would be four times the strength as the first dosage). He also recommended that I swim the sidestroke, while making sure my body was kept in that pelvic tilt position. The swimming felt wonderful, and combining the exercise with the Elavil lent me a good night's rest. For the first time in a long time, I felt good.

Soon after I started taking the whole tablet of Elavil, I developed terrible head noises. At night, it sounded like someone was downstairs hammering on the piano. When I was swimming in the pool, the sounds became even worse as I turned my head from side to side. It didn't take long for me to figure out that the Elavil was causing the noises. When I stopped taking the drug, the noises quit.

When I returned to the doctor and related my experience with the Elavil, he quite emphatically stated that it could not possibly be the drug that had caused the ringing in my ears. That said, he wrote out another prescription for more Elavil. I learned the hard way that drugs do, in fact, cause ringing of the ears. I was smart enough to dispose of the Elavil, and I convinced him to try something else. This time the drug was called Sinaquan.

Then, I recalled that my mother had been afflicted with ringing ears. Every morning, she would get up, take two Bufferin tablets and soak in a hot tub, just so she could get moving with her osteoporosis. She never did figure out that it was probably the Bufferin that caused her ear troubles.

As I concentrated on maintaining this unnatural pelvic tilt position, other problems began to develop. Pains shot down my legs and into my feet, and my entire right side began to hurt. I complained to the doctor at the pain clinic, who thought that I would be a good candidate to try out a new idea he'd come up with. He didn't tell me how new it was or what would be involved.

I agreed to be hospitalized. There were no X-rays or any other diagnostic tests this time. The transporter rushed me down a variety of long corridors, while once again, I wished I were unconscious. I was placed on a table with a gap in the middle that left the lumbar section of my back exposed. I was not given any explanation of what would take place next. It seemed like all the doctors associated with the pain clinic were in that room watching and I felt like I was the guinea pig of the day. I was stretched out, then slammed from underneath in the middle of my back with some object, and that was it. Then for two weeks, I was supposed to lie on a rolled-up blanket that was to be placed under my lower back.

Thankfully, I did not spend the entire day in that position, because it probably would have crippled me. I was allowed to walk to a pool that was heated to 100 degrees, where I waded around for an hour every day. That was a wonderful luxury. Warm water is simply the best relaxant, I've found. In addition, it took all of the weight off my spine. I'd sink down in the water up to my neck and watch while other patients, much worse off than I, were lowered into the water. It made me realize how lucky I was in comparison to them.

It was a very large hospital, obviously. Not every hospital has a swimming pool. The first time, I was accompanied by a nurse who showed me the blue lines painted on the corridor floor. We followed the lines to the pool room, where I was given a paper bathing suit. Since I was on no medication, there was no danger of falling, and the nurses allowed me to walk this long distance alone after I learned the way. The long walk and gentle exercise felt good and helped break the monotony of just lying in bed all day. My doctor would prescribe no drugs or sleeping pills, but instead suggested that I read, and explained to me how to make a pillow stand on end to support a book so that I could read while flat on my back.

The nurses were particularly friendly in this hospital. They loved to congregate in my room to watch one of their favorite soap shows, *The Young and the Restless*. Most patients were busy eating lunch and I enjoyed their company very much. It was amusing to observe how theses gals lived vicariously through the cast of crazy characters in a soap opera.

They also confided bits of their personal lives to me, along with a few complaints about patients. They were very friendly, compassionate nurses, dearly appreciated by their patients. Many recipients of their personal touches even promised gifts, although they usually never delivered.

"I know why," I told them. "Patients are usually so drugged up that they don't remember what they say!"

On one occasion, a nurse admired my watch, and I told her that I would buy one just like it for her when I got home. I finally recalled the conversation about three weeks after I left the hospital. I must admit that I never did buy that watch for her.

Although it was an uneventful, restful stay, the hospitalization and experimental treatment cost a lot of money. To this day, I still think the doctor should return my money for using me as a guinea pig for his ridiculous experiment. I am thankful that at least my back was not further damaged. Needless to say, it didn't help one bit.

At times, my family (and even me, on occasion) doubted the seriousness of my back problem and actually insinuated that maybe my problem was all in my head. I'll admit, it certainly seemed nutty to continue seeking a cure for my seemingly incurable condition, but I was convinced my injury was real.

I had even spent an hour with a psychiatrist while I was in the hospital. Most of that time though, I felt *I* was counseling *him* on spiritual matters. He had left a good church, had put God on the shelf, and was going the way of the world, living the good life that doctors can afford. But living for himself had left him with an emptiness inside. I could sense his longing for the peace and joy I talked about. For some reason, people think if you live a godly life, you won't be happy. I was always happy, in spite of the fact that I was dealing with what I thought was a mountain of a problem that my doctors refused to even acknowledge.

This psychiatrist asked me what I thought a back looked like.

"A chicken neck," was my answer. That satisfied him. He is the one doctor who never sent me a bill.

Traction

Yet another orthopedist put me in the hospital for traction. I was admitted late in the day, so there was no meal tray ordered for me. I was so hungry at 4:00 a.m., so I wandered out to the nurses' desk, hoping they would give me something to eat, maybe just a cracker. There was nothing.

I was hooked up to traction the next day. For anyone who doesn't know, low back traction uses weights on pulleys, attached by straps to a belt worn around the pelvis to pull or stretch muscles. In my case, I had a belt around the pelvic area and the weights gave a light tug. Actually, it was quite comfortable.

However, being immobilized by traction produces some of its own problems. Without any movement, it seems like the body's plumbing doesn't work too well. The hospital's answer was to provide laxatives, in this case, Milk of Magnesia. That stuff never worked for me, so my husband brought my own brand from home and I hid it.

The nurse never found the laxatives, but she did find my jar of vitamins. She gave me a dubious look, then questioned me sternly, "What are these?"

"Those are my vitamins," I answered confidently. I had learned by then to demonstrate some of my own authority. After all, patients have some rights.

Some vitamin tablets do look like prescription drugs, but she simply tossed the bottle back into the drawer with disgust.

After about the 12th day, that crazy feeling in my back disappeared. The doctor decided that two weeks had been long enough and sent me home. Unfortunately, the lack of pain did not last. I tried to be very careful, but I guess more time was needed for a complete healing.

Sometimes, after being so disappointed over yet another failed attempt at a cure, I would feel like crying. But I was determined not to wallow in self-pity. Instead, I'd go shopping. I would buy attractive clothing that would draw attention to my outside instead of my inside. I don't know if my family ever knew how poorly I felt. The shopping sprees, indeed, lifted my spirits. I thank God that my back problem was not completely debilitating, and I always reminded myself of the story about the little boy who felt sad, because he had no shoes, until he saw a man who had no feet.

I wore the brace I had been given years ago for a number of weeks and I learned to keep my back supported all the time. I even installed a home traction unit, but I still fought that nagging pressure and pain at night. In the hospital, a drug had been given so that my muscles would relax. Alas, none of the orthopedists I visited would prescribe any drugs for me, so I usually watched TV until I was able to fall asleep.

About this time, my husband and I met an ex-marine on the beach in Florida. He seemed to be very strong and he looked the picture of health. As we chatted with him, we were surprised to learn that he had a back problem similar to mine. He told us that his doctors were always trying to tell him that it was all in his head. I had certainly experienced the same thing. It really angered me when I could not convince any doctor that there was indeed something wrong with my back, but when I think back now, discrediting me was their way of letting me know that they, as doctors, were simply not interested, period, and would I please stay out of their offices.

The Chiropractor, the Neurosurgeon, and the Spinal Headache

I found that chiropractors were much different from medical doctors. They were always interested in scheduling another appointment for me. Sometimes their treatments helped, sometimes they didn't; and sometimes they even did a little damage. Unlike the doctors, the chiropractors acknowledged there was a problem and that it was curable with more and more of their treatments.

Months and years went by while I sought out treatments. After one visit to a chiropractor, he convinced me that a disc was the problem. I patiently waited three weeks for another visit with a neurosurgeon. When he saw my record of office visits and treatments, he decided to order a discogram.

I was admitted to a local hospital with the usually prescribed chest X-ray and blood work. I kept telling them that there was nothing wrong with my lungs, but as far as they were concerned, it was customary procedure. The actual discogram was very painful as dye was injected around the disc in question. I was once again wheeled back to my room on a gurney and instructed to remain in bed for 24 hours.

When the doctor visited me that evening, he told me I was to be discharged in the morning. He said I had the discs of a 15-year-old.

Being a neurosurgeon, he also said, "There is nothing more I can do for you. You have a lot of money [I don't know how he came up with that], and I will make arrangements for an appointment with another neurosurgeon at the Mayo Clinic."

I argued, "But neurosurgeons are surgeons like yourself. You have no interest in anything that doesn't require surgery." He sheepishly agreed. "I'll pass on that suggestion, but thank you, anyway."

He did not exhibit the least bit of interest in me or in my back problem when he learned that an operation was not necessary. When will I ever learn?

A nurse told me that I could get up to use the bathroom before going to sleep. That was a big mistake. Putting all the blame on the nurse would not be fair, because I just didn't want to use that awful bedpan! What I didn't know hurt me, and I suffered the consequences. It is necessary, and absolutely mandatory, to lie flat for 24 hours after any spinal injection, *period*. Of course, this was my first experience with a spinal, and as I've noted before, it seems like I must learn everything the hard way. I left the hospital the next day with a doozy of a headache.

I phoned the doctor about my wincing headache, and he advised, "You have what we call a spinal headache. I can admit you to the hospital again, where you can lie flat for 24 hours."

"No, thanks," I quickly answered. "I will make arrangements at home." I surprised myself!

Now, I am always on the lookout for self-treatments. I plan to avoid any hospital treatments for my back in the future.

I don't know how or when I acquired my own little bedpan, but I decided to put it to use that day. My family agreed to help me on the condition that there would be no BMs. They were lucky. I had already been to the bathroom before I'd called the doctor. As long as I laid flat, I felt okay. One day of bed rest was all I needed to get rid of the headache.

My daughter also suffered terribly from a spinal headache after she delivered her third child with the help of an epidural, which is an anesthetic given by injection directly into the spinal cord. A nurse told her that she could sit up to eat her evening meal. She rested as much as possible when she returned home, but the never-ending duties of caring for three small children never afforded her the opportunity to stay off her feet long enough. Her headache lasted for three weeks.

A spinal headache is hard to describe. If you ever get one, you will discover how painful it is. In her case, it was so unnecessary. Nurses should be instructed to ask if a new mother has had a spinal injection before they advise her to sit up and eat or use the bathroom. So many things are learned the hard way.

Back Survivors

There are valuable lessons I learned too late to help with my own back problem, but my hope is that they will bring some comfort or help to someone else. I agree with Dr. Robert Shuler, "Everyone has problems. If you don't, you are probably dead."

There are only two women I know who have completely recovered from a back injury similar to mine. The first woman was in such pain. She told me that she practically crawled into the orthopedist's office. She was hospitalized for one month. The doctor's orders were for her to remain in bed continually—no sitting, walking, or using the bathroom.

That was the same woman who had advised me to go to her orthopedist, and I guess that's when the idea was conceived that I should be treated and cured in a hospital. Her doctor was the first doctor I consulted with about my back problem. He stared at me blankly and told me he didn't remember any such treatment. He thought I did not need to be hospitalized.

With the tremendous rise in the cost of hospital treatments, and the dictates from the insurance companies, perhaps he felt he could no longer justify a month's hospitalization. After all, taking up a hospital bed for that long, just to rest, probably seemed outrageously expensive and unnecessary. But believe me, in the end, it would have been the least expensive way to go.

The second woman I spoke with was about 45 years old when she injured her back picking up a heavy object. It was very painful and her medical doctor wisely gave her some pain medicine and told her to rest. And rest she did. She took three months off from her office job and stayed at home all the while. Yes, it was boring, she said. She would rest a little, and then walk a little. She never sat for long, and there was no bending, no exercises, and no physical work at all. Her back healed completely, probably for the price of an office visit and a little bottle of pills.

Taking charge of your own treatment, like this woman did, is very hard to do. It isn't easy to say, "No, I can't do that, can't go there, can't sit in church, can't play golf, can't travel, can't do the laundry. I am going to do nothing but rest," when all the while you look perfectly healthy. Through all these years of doctor visits and hospitalizations, I did look robust and perfectly healthy. It's no wonder the doctors didn't take me seriously.

It Takes Time

While I was waiting to see one doctor, a young patient of his stumbled into the waiting room. She was clearly suffering with back pain. Her husband and two small children were with her. She had no appointment, but asked if she could see the doctor because she thought it was an emergency. She had been his patient for 17 years.

He would not see her, and I heard him call out, "Tell her to go to an orthopedist."

This is the same doctor who put me in the hospital with my gallbladder problem. My back had bothered me a lot then while I lay in that bed for so long.

On one of his morning visits, I said to him, "If I knew then what I know now about a back injury, I could have cured myself in three months just by resting, doing gentle walking, doing a little sitting, and perhaps taking a muscle relaxant for a restful night's sleep."

He looked at me in surprise and said, "You're absolutely right!"

Yet when a patient of his had asked for his help, he refused to even see her or to offer any help whatsoever, even though she'd been his patient for years.

Chiropractors, medical doctors, orthopedists, and neurosurgeons all have visual aids in one form or another that depict the vertebrae and discs. But they rarely discuss the ligaments that attach bone to bone, or the tendons that attach muscle to bone, neither of which shows up on X-rays. Those cords run the full length of the spine, and are fashioned in such a way to allow flexibility of the spine, while adhering to the bone. When an injury takes place, ligaments can be pulled slightly off the bone. It takes a lot of time for ligaments and tendons to heal, because of the complexity of the spine.

Most doctors will prescribe exercises and rest. That's just like taking a broken arm out of a cast, exercising it, and then putting the cast back on again. It doesn't make sense and I am sure it doesn't facilitate healing. That's why there are so many people today with what they call "bad backs."

I never knew the answer could be so simple: The back will adjust itself if you just give it time. When an injury is old, one doctor explained, ligaments will become like old elastic, and a complete cure is impossible. There are cases where discs can be so damaged, or vertebrae can be fractured. In those cases, surgery is certainly beneficial, even necessary. But there is a very low percentage of back problems that need surgery, or even need to be diagnosed with an expensive CAT scan or MRI.

It has been more than 20 years now, and I have learned to live with my back problem. Unfortunately, I had to learn the hard way by trying every method that *didn't* work, and paying for it! I learned to finish a hot shower with a very cold one and not to do any strenuous work or play after a hot shower, when the muscles are relaxed. I also learned to support my back with pillows and comfortable chairs. I also choose to live with a grateful heart.

Comfort for My Aching Back

I have tried every kind of bed, treatment, and medical contraption you can imagine in hopes of finding some comfort. For the last 20 years, I have kept notes on the numerous suggestions that have been recommended, as well as the sources of further back irritation.

<u>Beds:</u> I took one doctor's advice and bought a very expensive, extra firm, king-sized mattress. It was so hard, neither my husband nor I could sleep on it. I bought a traction outfit, slept in a hospital bed loaned to me by a funeral parlor, and tried a waterbed with baffles and one without baffles. I bought one of those expensive Niagara beds that have a vibrator and can elevate the head or foot. After everything I tried, I still had that nagging pain and feeling of pressure on my lower back.

<u>Ice:</u> I learned that heat and vibrators relax the muscles, so the spine can adjust itself. Ice reduces the inflammation in the nerves and tightens up the ligaments.

Many times, ice has been prescribed for my back. But it's almost impossible to lie comfortably on a bag filled with ice. So I invented my own ice bag. I folded a thick washcloth, soaked it with water, placed it in a zipped plastic bag, and stuck it in the freezer. The next day, voila, a nice, flat ice bag. It stays frozen for about 20 minutes, which is just about the time needed. Plus, it can be used over and over again simply by refreezing it. My self-created ice bag doesn't contour to the body as well as the marketed soft ice packs, but you're not supposed to lie on the soft ones. I'm very proud of my handiwork!

One chiropractor suggested slipping a soft ice bag on my back under my clothing, right at the waist line. It worked. Ice seemed to freeze the pain away for a short while.

<u>Pillows:</u> I also bought and made all sorts of pillows that gave my back support while sitting. In church last year, a helpful woman seated behind me handed me a tiny pillow filled with just a little bit of air. It was the most comfortable thing I had ever used. It folded flat when the air was let out, and could be conveniently carried in a purse. I tried to find the manufacturer in California, but I was unsuccessful.

<u>Hanging Contraptions:</u> A chiropractor consultant who was handling his own back problem in his own way showed me his orthopod. It was designed so that a person could hang upside down from the hips. I wrapped my legs around these two padded bars, and then, by giving myself a push over the seat, I found myself hanging by my thighs upside-down. It was great for the thoracic area, and I'm sure for a few years it helped to relieve the tension.

<u>Cars:</u> As opposed to church pew construction, auto manufacturers definitely have comfort in mind when they design car seats. At least the immediate reaction to most car seats is one of comfort. But they are not necessarily comfortable in the long run for those of us with back problems. Most seats create a cradle effect, allowing passengers to sit back and relax. But without proper support, over time, tension is created in the lower back. I tried the lumbar expansion featured in certain makes of cars, thinking it would be the answer. But my Oldsmobile seat curved in the wrong direction! It did not support my back—in fact, it did just the opposite.

I once heard a discussion between a couple of traveling salesmen who'd spent a lot of time in their cars. The obvious limp by one of the men revealed that his back was really bothering him.

The second man asked, "What make of car do you drive?"

The first man pointed proudly to his nice, new Chevrolet.

The second man replied, "There's the cause of your back problem. I used to drive one, too."

I'm convinced that there is a right time for everything. One day, soon after hearing this conversation, General Motors just happened to send me a questionnaire requesting my opinion of my new Oldsmobile. I was more than happy to oblige! I reported to the company that their seats were not comfortable for me, and that they were not made to support the lumbar section of the back. I also related the conversation I'd heard between the two salesmen. (I never did think there was much difference between a Chevy and an Olds anyway.) It surprised me when General Motors sent me a very prompt reply thanking me for my response to their questionnaire.

Now, I don't want to take all the credit for it, but I did notice in the latest Oldsmobile we purchased, the seats were much more comfortable and I no longer needed a pillow to help support my back.

Pickups: My brand new red pickup truck was so sharp. It had a bench-style seat that allowed me to sit upright with my feet on the floor. It was quite comfortable, although it was something of a bouncy ride. I shocked some of my friends who lived in rather upscale neighborhoods when I offered to pick them up. When I showed up in my red pickup, I think they were embarrassed—they would sort of duck down, so that their neighbors would not see them.

I know for many it was their very first ride in a pickup truck. I'd say, "Nice seats, don't you think?"

"Very comfortable," they'd answer.

"Kinda fun, huh?"

"Oh, yes," they'd admit.

I still maintain that you haven't lived till you have ridden in a pickup.

Chairs: For the most part, the backs of office chairs are great. They are usually adjustable and can be moved to support the lumbar area of the back. I find I can sit comfortably for hours in an office chair.

I tried one of those office chairs that you kneel on, but my knees did not like it.

Dining or kitchen chairs are not made for comfort. Typically, when you dine, you sit up straight and lean over. This is tiring as it puts a strain on the lower back. It's just not a comfortable position for anyone with a serious back problem.

Forget the easy chairs or stuffed sofas. You're better off on the floor.

Most medical literature on the back will advise you to beg, buy, or borrow a rocking chair. Therefore, I have one in every room of my home. I've found the older the chair, the better. Unless you have a very short body, the armrests on most modern chairs are useless and do not help relieve tension in the back.

For years, I have found that lying flat on the floor is the most comfortable position. Not too graceful, but it sure feels the best. I also do a lot of stretching exercises right on my living room floor, which entails no purchase or cost whatsoever!

A Patient's Perspective

The Waiting Game

One afternoon, I happened to be one of about eight people waiting in a dermatologist's office, where I was entertaining myself by reading an old magazine. I glanced at my watch and commented to the person beside me, "I must be next. I'm the 3:15."

"I'm a 3:15, too," she asserted.

Then two others joined the chorus.

Recently, I received a reminder in the mail from a doctor's office that verified my 1:00 p.m. appointment with the doctor. The letter requested that if, for any reason, I was unable to keep this appointment, to please notify the office. The note went on to ask that I arrive at the office 5 to 10 minutes before my scheduled time.

I'm always thankful for these reminders, especially this one, since I'd made the appointment two months earlier. Have you ever arrived at an office a day late, or perhaps a day early? I was 20 minutes late once and my visit was postponed for two weeks!

I obediently arrived at this doctor's office at 12:50, where I found another patient patiently waiting for *her* 1:00 appointment. I was ushered into the examining room at 1:20.

When will I ever learn to take the waiting room reading material with me when I'm left to wait even longer in the examining room? Fifteen minutes is a long time to stare at Q-Tips, tongue depressors, drug samples, and examining gloves.

The truth is, the anxiety caused by waiting can cause an abnormal blood pressure reading. The first reading may not be revealed to you, the patient, because if it's high you'll go from being anxious to really worrying, and that will cause the blood pressure to go higher yet. A second reading will usually be more accurate.

The visit I was making on this day was with a plastic surgeon. He sat on a stool with his face about a foot away from mine scrutinizing all the wrinkles on my face and probably thought, "I'll be able to retire early if I get this job!"

I'm vain, but not that vain, and I prefer to live with my wrinkles. Like my sister says, "People like you because you have more wrinkles than they do."

My family doctor had suggested a visit with this doctor because of numbness in my thumb. This is one doctor who said, in so many words, that the nerves would heal all by themselves, and he was right. He almost said those magical words, "You will get better."

One time, after waiting in an orthopedist's office for 90 exhausting minutes, the receptionist informed the three of us diehards that the doctor had been called out of the office to handle an emergency. She then asked us to come to the desk so we could reschedule our appointments. We did so reluctantly. Then we could come back and wait some more. Wait, wait, wait. Sometimes, being a *patient* patient is difficult indeed.

X-rays

It seems that these days doctors don't want to take the time to use that good old-fashioned stethoscope. EKGs and chest X-rays are ordered instead. I asked my doctor once if it was possible to discover most irregularities in the circulation system in fairly healthy adults with a stethoscope. He maintained it was possible. Most problems with the lungs can be detected by stethoscope as well. So, I always opt to go that route during my annual physical. I know it is more technically advanced to have an electrocardiogram, but someone still has to operate the machine and read and type the report. Mistakes can be made either way, but I prefer the personal touch of a physician. When a stethoscope is used, only the doctor knows for sure what he hears. Of course, one of the benefits of an EKG or X-ray is that it produces a copy as a permanent record.

An X-ray is actually just an exposure on film or on a plate. It is made by an X-ray machine that shoots electrons throughout the body through to a metallic plate on which photographic film is placed. X-ray technicians and radiologists, however, are human beings. And, as we all know, "to err is human."

In the case of a very close friend, her mammogram X-rays were delivered to the doctor and both the radiologist *and* the doctor misread the plates. This was a very serious mistake, as cancer was involved, and a lumpectomy was performed. Soon after, my friend was advised by another doctor to go to a university hospital to see an oncologist of some repute who specialized in mastectomies.

This doctor was not satisfied with merely reading the radiologist's report. He demanded to see the original X-ray plates. It was then that this specialist discovered that there was even more cancer in the breast than had been noted, and he performed the necessary full mastectomy. I shudder to think what would have happened had only the lumpectomy been performed. We can all learn from this mistake. Always insist that the doctor personally review the X-ray plates with you.

My friend has fully recovered and she is considered a cancer survivor. Now she fortifies her diet with known cancer fighting vitamins, namely C and E, beta carotene, and selenium. She is convinced that all the chemicals in the air and water, along with pesticides and food preservatives cause cancer, and she may be right.

Acting upon what she knows and believes, she plants a garden to grow her own veggies and she buys organic food whenever possible. Keeping the immune system healthy is necessary to ward off any disease, especially cancer.

Most experienced X-ray technicians can tell right away if there is anything abnormal. Of course, they are not permitted to tell patients. On one occasion, I was smart enough to remember to ask my doctor if he would give the okay for the technician to let me know if everything was normal. He granted my request. When the technician read the plates, he immediately reported to me that nothing was wrong. Everything was normal. That way, I didn't have to be concerned over the weekend.

My friend wasn't that fortunate. A lump was found on her breast. Her medical doctor sent her to an oncologist who did a biopsy. She waited a week for his office to call to report the results. She suffered through many anxious days as she waited and waited. Finally, on Friday morning, she called the doctor's office to learn if the results were available. "Yes," they reported, "the results were in, but the doctor was out of town for the weekend."

She begged the office nurse, "Could you please tell me what the test revealed?"

The very apologetic nurse replied, "I'm sorry, I can't tell you. The doctor will have to see you."

"When is the earliest appointment available?" she asked.

The nurse understood how disappointed this patient was and explained, "The earliest time for you to see the doctor will be next Tuesday."

Her worrying went into third gear. She assumed that if there was nothing wrong, the nurse could have told her.

Finally, in the doctor's presence, she learned the lump was benign. She had nothing to fear. Benign is a wonderful word to hear for anyone threatened with cancer, but my friend was so irate with her doctor for making her wait so long for the good news that she had a hard time even comprehending it, let alone feeling relieved.

Nothing to fear but fear itself? Not necessarily true when you are waiting for test results that could possibly reveal cancer, or in her case, the absence of cancer.

The Worried Patient

I suppose if we are honest enough to admit it, we all worry, and we all become anxious when we enter the hospital or the doctor's office, or if we are waiting for test results. And I think we can all agree: Worrying does not do one bit of good. Many things that we worry about, for the most part, never take place. In the meantime, worrying about them zaps our energy and leaves us feeling distressed and uneasy.

Occasional feelings of doubt when our health is threatened are perfectly normal. It's when we dwell on those troubling feelings continually that we endanger our own well-being, and we wear out our friends who have enough troubles of their own and don't need to listen to ours.

An acquaintance I'll call Mary worries about everything, especially her health. She uses her blood pressure kit, she takes her temperature, and she weighs herself daily (although she never tells us how much she weighs). When her husband died about eight years ago, she worried herself right into the doctor's office.

After all of the routine tests were completed, her family doctor, who understood his patient, also ordered a CAT scan to satisfy her. Well, Mary almost died when a spot was discovered on her liver. After carefully examining the plates, it was determined the spot was benign.

Having nothing to fear as far as her health was concerned, she worried needlessly about her finances, her family relationships, the upcoming elections, the weather, and any other thing she could not control. It's a good thing she never learned about our national debt.

Finally, after years of counseling, she seemed to be reasonably happy. Then, for some unexplained reason, she began to lose weight. The same doctor repeated another complete physical and ordered another CAT scan.

Why does it take a week to get the results for such a simple test? she began to wonder. It was beyond her comprehension. Seven days is a long time to worry about something major like this.

Finally, a call came from the doctor's office requesting her to return the next day. She was told by the person on the phone that the CAT scan had revealed a tumor on her liver. Needless to say, she didn't sleep a wink that night. Too busy planning her funeral. She called one of her sons to accompany her.

In the examination room, she could barely sit still. She stared at the doorknob for what seemed to her an eternity, waiting for it to turn.

When the doctor finally entered, he asked, "Why are you here?"

She was taken aback by his question, and looked blankly at her doctor. Then she said, with great emotion, "Your office called me and told me that I have a tumor on my liver!"

"Oh Mary, I think there must be some mistake. I didn't ask anyone to call you."

Acutely aware that there had been a major mistake in communication, the doctor put his arm around her, and together, they viewed the plates of the CAT scan. They then compared the results to the previous CAT scan and they observed that the appearance of that spot had not changed. She had been so convinced that she was going to die, it was hard for her brain to grasp the fact that, indeed, she was going to live.

Her doctor prescribed a mild sedative and after she had finally composed herself, she walked out of the doctor's office greatly relieved, but duly aggravated. It is quite a jolt to be told you have a tumor on your liver and suspect the worst, only to be told days later that there is nothing wrong. The doctor apologized profusely on behalf of the person who had made that unfortunate call.

Weeks later, Mary was back in a counselor's office learning how to deal with and eliminate anger. It is a fact that it takes the same amount of energy to brood in anger as it does to run a race. Her counselor very wisely suggested forgiveness. Although she did have a legitimate reason for feeling anger toward the person who had mistakenly phoned her, he did not intentionally mean to harm her. Her doctor had graciously apologized, so she finally agreed to let it go. Yes, that's easier said than done, but sometimes that's the best way—just let go of it.

Our First Emergency

When my son was nine years old, he climbed up into a willow tree after he heard his little kitten, named Kitty, crying in her pathetic, helpless way. It seemed as if she didn't know how to get down from the tree, and she was afraid to jump. The limb Kitty was sitting on wasn't very high, but she sat out on the very end of it. When my son was almost able to reach her, the limb broke and so did my son's arm. I heard the limb crash and I heard his scream.

My heart sank as I watched my husband carry his limp body inside our farmhouse. The boy was in shock. My husband and I both stared at each other until he finally had the presence of mind to blurt out, "Call the doctor!"

"Which one?" I wondered out loud.

We both examined the limp limb. "The bone doctor," he declared with great urgency.

Until this time, we had never encountered any medical emergencies. We didn't even have a family doctor at that time. I fumbled around with the telephone book, looking for the name of the doctor who had done a beautiful job patching the broken leg of one of our friends. Even though this was our first experience with a broken bone, we knew it was serious and we wanted a specialist. We were thankful it was not a compound fracture, with bone protruding through the skin, but it was quite evident from the way his wrist and hand hung that both of the bones in his arm were broken.

Eventually, I recognized the doctor's name in the phonebook and dialed his office. I demanded to speak with the doctor himself because I considered this a dire emergency. I had no idea that patients rarely, if ever, speak directly with a doctor on the phone, because this means interrupting the doctor's regular office visits.

However, this orthopedic doctor took my call and immediately took control. I knew by the tone of his voice that he would not do anything for my son until morning. We reluctantly followed his advice and admitted my son to the hospital. His arm was packed in ice to keep the swelling down until morning when the doctor would set the bone. I stayed in the room with my son that evening until he was sleeping soundly.

After I left him, a sick baby was placed in the room with him. He told me the next day that the continual crying had kept him awake most of the night. I was so sorry I had left him. Had I stayed, I could have insisted that the baby be moved to another room. This was my first experience leaving a child in a hospital, and I learned how important it is to stay by your child's side.

When I arrived at the hospital early the next morning, I heard this pathetic crying coming from my son's room. Once again, my heart skipped a beat or two as I ran to him, only to find his bed empty. It was the pitiful crying of the baby in the other bed I had heard. At first, I felt like picking her up and comforting her. However, on second thought, when I looked at her runny nose, I was reminded that children are germ-infested little creatures. I decided to leave her to the nurses' care.

Minutes later, my son was wheeled in with his arm in a cast, all ready to go home. He experienced his first wheelchair ride out the front exit. He was so glad to get out of that hospital, and his first request was to visit his grandmother, who lived nearby, so she could see his new cast.

The orthopedic doctor we had contacted turned out to be very thorough. He ordered that the arm be X-rayed every two weeks. Our son handled his cast very cautiously—that is until his first visit with the doctor. There in the waiting room, he saw a rambunctious little boy swinging his cast around, grabbing toys, and playing quite normally. Following his example, my son threw away his sling and no longer felt it was necessary to baby his arm.

By the end of the sixth week, I decided to allow him to go to camp as we had planned. After all, the cast was to be removed by the end of the seventh week. The cast was really quite mutilated when we arrived at the hospital after a week of camp. The doctor was a bit disgusted.

"Couldn't you control him any better than that?" he asked angrily, using a few choice words that I will not print.

Knowing by now that this doctor took his work very seriously, I thought it best to just sit quietly and let him vent his temper. Besides, I was fascinated by watching him use that little saw to remove the cast. To demonstrate just how unhappy he was with me, the doctor slung the cast clear across the room where it slid under another examining table and struck the wall with a loud crash. It startled me, and one of the nurses was so frightened that she left the room. He ordered one last X-ray and then left the room without another word to me.

This bone doctor took all precautions necessary to ensure that the bones he set healed perfectly. Many of his patients thank him for it, including us. He never won any congeniality awards, but he gained an excellent reputation for his remarkable surgeries. I was particularly thankful that I had chosen this brilliant doctor to set my son's arm.

Some 20 years later, when my son broke his ankle, I knew exactly which doctor to recommend.

Hospital Visitors

How I wish hospital visitors would be a little more sensitive and thoughtful while visiting patients recovering from surgery. If they really want their visit to be appreciated, I suggest waiting until day three or four after surgery.

Just let me sleep, was my wish as a patient.

Once, when I was recovering from surgery, not to mention a sleepless night, I asked for a pain shot. Lunch was over and the meal tray had been cleared away. I asked to have the drapes drawn, and I thought, ah, now I will get some sleep. Ha! Think again! A perfectly nice, friendly acquaintance entered my room. She seemed totally unaware that my eyes weren't able to focus. She stayed and stayed and stayed, talking about people I knew, people I did not know (or care to know), television shows, obituaries, the price of gas, and the next person she would visit in the hospital that day. When there was nothing more to be said, she was still saying it. My mouth had become parched and dry just listening to her. She offered me a sip of water as if she were an angel of mercy.

I learned from this unwelcome visit that if you want your visit to be appreciated, wait until the patient wants to talk, and then just listen. The hospital itself is a whole new environment and a huge topic for conversation, especially when you are confined to one.

Contrary to what our well-meaning friends believe, patients very seldom get lonely in a hospital. Actually, after surgery, most patients don't need any additional stimulation in this time of recovery. The hospital routine is quite enough excitement. What the body usually needs is healing sleep or quiet rest to aid in the healing process.

But everyone likes to know they are loved. Flowers, cards, gifts, and short visits are always appreciated. With so many outpatient treatments these days, your cards might as well go to the patient's home address. I like to receive live plants in the springtime so that they can be planted outdoors when I get home.

One of the nicest gifts I ever received was from my own mother. I was recovering from a *tympanyplasty*, which is the medical term for an eardrum repair. It was one of my first experiences with any kind of drug or anesthetic, and that whopping shot of Valium in the hip given at about 8:00 in the morning really knocked me out. I limped for three days afterwards. To my knowledge, that was the only anesthetic used during the surgery, except for the local around the ear for the skin graft. I don't recall being transported back to my room, and I slept through lunch. I was completely unaware of the concerned friends who visited me that day.

Around 5:30 in the evening, a nurse said, "Wouldn't you like to eat a little something?"

I thought it was lunch, and I ate a few slices of canned peaches before falling back to sleep. Then, at 8:30 in the evening, I woke up mighty hungry. I rolled over and stared at a lovely fresh piece of homemade buttered Beirawicka, which is a German Christmas bread my mom baked every year made with prunes, raisins, walnuts, and filberts. It is truly a labor of love, requiring about five hours of preparation. Every delicious bite was savored. Then I slept again.

Now that I've survived many more hospital stays, I know how hard it is to get anything to eat on the surgical floor after the meal trays are gone. I can't wait to get to heaven to say, "Thanks again, Mom." I want her to know just how much I appreciated that slice of bread. What a simple but understanding act of a mother's love!

7

Giving Life

My First Baby

Not everyone sought the care of an OB/GYN for prenatal care and delivery during the late 40s when I had my first child. It is interesting to compare the differences of giving birth then with today's advanced knowledge and technology. Perhaps you'll agree, you can't quite call it *advanced*. Sometimes it seems to me like more of a return to the natural way.

My family doctor delivered my first child. He and his wife were great advocates of health food, and he advised all of his patients to be very conscious of their diets, especially while carrying a baby. He used to say that babies are made out of the food the mother eats. He even advised me to eat Pablum for breakfast, and I followed his advice. Yuck! This doctor really took to heart the old proverb:

> *"The whiter the bread,*
> *The sooner you're dead."*

He suggested that I avoid all foods containing white flour or white sugar. That, in itself, eliminated all junk food. It also produced a very skinny baby. My newborn son looked like a little old man, so full of wrinkles. He was just a bundle of bones without an ounce of fat on him.

Looking back, I'm very surprised that this doctor, who was so nutrition conscious, didn't recommend breast feeding. I believe that mother's milk is the best and most beneficial food a baby will ever get. He, like most doctors during the Second World War, may have encouraged bottle feeding so that we women could get back to the factories. Rosie the Riveter was probably one of the first women to bottle feed her baby!

I missed much of my son's birth. Childbirth classes for expectant couples were not in existence at that time. My husband sat at my side for part of the time while I was in labor, but he was not able to offer any instruction or comfort. Finally, he was told to wait in the room for expecting fathers.

There was no coaching by nurses or doctors. Ether was administered to put me under completely, and I was unable to assist in the birthing process. Forceps were used to pull the baby out. The baby slept for a week, and I didn't even get to see the color of his eyes. All of the mothers were given ether as an anesthetic, so that made for a very quiet nursery. We could barely wake our babies to feed them!

My baby was born at two o'clock in the morning, but I did not see or hold him until 10 o'clock the next morning. The feeling of my newborn son, so warm and soft when he was placed in my arms, will linger with me for the rest of my life. I am sure that other mothers feel the same way. He barely opened his eyes the whole time I was in the hospital. I missed his first cry as a new life being born into the world.

I am glad that the fathers of today can be such an integral part of the delivery process, and that they can experience the miracle of the first moments of birth. As for my husband, he waited, with great anticipation, for four long hours, until the doctor made his customary appearance and congratulated him on the birth of his son. He didn't get to see me or the baby until visiting hours the next day.

My dad, who was a real corker, made up a story about having to go back to Chicago, and said that he would not be able to see his grandson for a long time. He begged the nurses to let him hold the baby for a little while and they actually let him sit in a rocking chair and rock the baby for quite a while, thinking that they were doing this new grandpa a great favor.

Believe it or not, I remained in the hospital for 10 days. The baby was almost ready to crawl by that time! Not really. He was probably just waking up from the ether.

New mothers were treated like invalids at that time. We were even bathed by the nurses. Breast feeding was discouraged, denying us that special mother's pleasure, as well as healthy nourishment for our babies. There was one advantage to not nursing. It allowed us to get a whole night's sleep—something we would not get at home for quite a while.

The fun part of staying in the hospital was receiving gifts for the baby and for me from friends and relatives. One friend sent me a large bouquet of gladiolas. Glads are very pretty, but eventually my room began to smell like a funeral parlor.

It was a very happy day for my husband and me when I was wheeled out the front door of the hospital with our new baby in my arms. I'll never forget seeing the green leaves of the huge maple trees fully developed and covering the street like a tunnel. The miracle of Spring had taken place during those 10 days in the hospital. Now we were driving home with our own little miracle, a newborn baby.

My Baby's Baby

Ruthie, the youngest of my children, will always be referred to as "the baby." She gave birth at the ages of 28 and 32, in two distinctly different ways. The following is her description of the birthing process.

*

"I considered myself a by-product of the *natural* phenomena of the 1960s. Not that I went braless that often, or ate a strictly vegetarian diet, but I did believe that natural was best, if possible. Fresh food was better than prepared food, and fresh air, clean water, and fit bodies were the basis for a healthy life.

"So, when I became pregnant, I sought a female doctor who would help me to have a natural childbirth—as natural as it could be in a hospital, anyway. I wanted a female doctor because I felt that a female would instinctively know more about a woman's body than a male doctor would. This is a philosophy I still maintain today. My doctor was a small Filipino woman who spoke very little English and had a quiet, sincere, yet knowing way about her.

"While trying to get pregnant, she had explained to me, in just a few words, how delicate a woman's system is, and that just the *trying* is enough to upset the hormonal balance in a woman's reproductive system.

'Better to not try, and just have fun,' she told me.

"Through the years, I have witnessed many couples *try* to exhaustion, claim infertility in one spouse or the other, employ the use of artificial insemination, or adopt, and then quickly thereafter become pregnant with ease, without even *trying*.

"We took her advice and had lots of fun. The result, or maybe you could call it the consequence, of that fun is the birth I am about to describe.

"My water broke at about 5:00 a.m., and my husband and I packed our things for the drive from Brooklyn into Manhattan. I even stopped by my office to send out one last FedEx package before checking into the hospital.

"A male intern, with all the grace and tender care of a rhinoceros, examined me and reported that I was seven or eight centimeters dilated. I did not like being strapped to that monitor and I kept a lookout for my doctor. Eventually, she appeared masked between my legs, and she seemed to be holding something on my posterior. I asked her what she was doing. She held up a small plastic disc and said, 'This will prevent you from having hemorrhoids.'

"Now, I ask you, would a male doctor do that for you?

"A few seemingly short hours later, I was ready to push, but I was told to wait until I was moved to an operating room. Unfortunately, the hospital was busy that day and I was rolled into the hallway with my legs pulled up to my chest and my rear end in the air. I told my husband to pull the sheet over my head as I had another contraction. I gave birth at 2:05 p.m., about two minutes after being rolled into the delivery room.

"Fast-forward five years: We were living in a small town in New Jersey. We had practiced *not trying*, and we had quickly conceived. I happened to meet a midwife at the preschool my daughter attended, and I inquired about her services. Both my husband and I were self-employed at the time, so I was most interested in saving money, as well as an even more natural childbirth than the last. Plus, I figured that if I had the baby at home, I would at least be guaranteed a bed.

"I did meet with a local doctor who was affiliated with a hospital as back-up, just in case anything went wrong in labor. I probably would have lacked the confidence to go with a home birth with my first child, but feeling like I had some experience, and that things had gone relatively easily for me, I thought I could do it the second time around.

"What a different scene it was. My water broke at about 10:00 p.m. and my husband continued to lie on the floor watching Michael Jordan and the Bulls in the NBA finals. I called and told the midwife what had happened and I went to bed. She arrived around 4:00 a.m. with her assistant and she made some coffee right off the bat.

"I took a shower and laid on my bed, and I remember seeing her looking over the footboard at about 7:00 a.m. and saying, 'It's going to be very soon now.'

"'How do you know that?' I wanted to know.

"'I just know,' she said.

"Sure enough, at 8:01, my son fell to the floor. Not literally. As the midwife had explained earlier, when one has the freedom, one may assume any position during the birthing process. Unknowingly, I had assumed the praying position, on my knees at the edge of my bed, while I wrung my husband's hand nearly off of his arm.

"My husband cut the umbilical cord and I climbed into bed. My son was handed to me, and my daughter walked into the room at 8:05. She was thrilled to see her brand new little baby brother. A few days later, we planted the placenta under a Japanese maple tree in the yard. The midwife had told us that the placenta was loaded with nutrients. You can't get any more natural than that."

A Bouncing Baby Boy

This is the story my other daughter tells about her Caesarian birth experience at age 41.

"People used to tell me that it was more likely that I would be struck by lightening than to marry after age 40. Now, giving birth at age 41, I was completely overwhelmed. God does surprise us!

"While viewing the sonogram of our first child, the doctor pointed out a picture of a hand, and the sign of the *turtle*. It was a boy. He peeked around at a few other vital organs to see if all was tuned up and running fine. Then he pointed out a tiny sack of small calcified gallstones. He informed me that, no doubt, at a later date, the gallstones would have to be removed.

"The pregnancy progressed normally until the seventh month when a fibroid tumor that could cause premature labor was discovered. I was forced to spend two months in bed. At the end of the eighth month, I was allowed out of bed. However, I found it extremely difficult to go about my normal routine, because I was carrying what had now become a very large child.

"All of my muscles had been weakened from the extended bed rest. It was a first-class struggle just to get up and try to get a few things done around the house. I was tempted many times to crawl back in the sack and nap till dinner, but I knew that somehow I must develop the strength to care for this precious little bundle I was carrying.

"Because of my age, and the size of the baby, a caesarean section birth had been advised by my doctor. The night before my scheduled C-section, my husband and I had our last hurrah before our lives were to be changed forever. We strolled through our neighborhood shopping district and stopped for dinner at our favorite restaurant. I indulged and ordered a spicy southwestern salad. After dinner, we walked to the movie theater.

"The most recent sonogram had revealed that the baby had extra long femurs. That night, he had been kicking violently, as if to protest the spicy food I'd eaten, or so I thought. Right before reaching the theater, I began to experience unusual pain just above the baby's position. Still hopeful, we purchased tickets, thinking that the pain would subside, and we settled into seats close to the door.

"Very soon, the pain only got worse, so I whispered to my husband, 'Honey, you better get the car!' He understood and frantically rushed out of the theater. I sat on a step just inside the lobby, leaning back in pain.

"A young female usher asked? 'Are you okay?'

"In response, I wailed a loud, emphatic, 'Nooooo!'

"The usher, who was obviously frightened, stood helplessly nearby and watched with bulging eyes. She probably thought the baby was going to be delivered right then and there.

"After we returned home, I immediately called the doctor, who became very concerned. To him, the pain I described didn't sound like labor pains. He advised me to get to the hospital to have everything checked out.

"The nurse who examined me said, 'Honey, that's just your baby with those long legs kicking your ribs.'

"We returned home at 1:00 in the morning to get a few hours of sleep before reporting back to the hospital at 5:00 a.m. for our scheduled appointment.

"My husband wanted to be in the delivery room with me, so he donned the blue sterile gown, cap, and mask. Being 6'6" tall, the nurse kept a close eye on him. She asked him to hide behind a screen while the baby was taken from my belly, and while the fibroids were removed.

"She said to my husband, 'If you faint in here, there aren't enough of us to scrape you up off the floor.'

"He didn't have to wait long behind that screen until he heard the first cry of his big baby boy. He was the first one to hold him and the bonding between father and son began right there. Five days later, Mommy, Daddy, and baby were all back home.

"When my baby was three weeks old, I was sitting on the sofa nursing him when those sharp pains started again.

'Honey, it's not the baby this time,' I told my husband. 'It can't be, he's in my arms.'

"I recognized this pain as the same one I had experienced just before I'd had my C-section. Obviously, it wasn't a result of the baby kicking. It had to be something else. The pain was serious enough that I went straight to the emergency room. The doctors found that certain liver enzymes were elevated and they determined that it was a gallbladder attack.

"I checked into a major research hospital for gallbladder surgery and made the routine stops in the laboratory, X-ray room, and surgeon's office. Plus, I visited the delivery wing to pump my breasts. The doctors were not sure if they wanted to proceed with the operation because the X-rays showed a spot on my lung. I was sent back for additional X-rays, all the while hoping I would not have another painful attack. The surgeons finally decided to go ahead with surgery as scheduled, since the spot was only visible from the front view.

"It was at that point I discovered the X-ray department had recorded my age as two months, and the laboratory had recorded my age as 98 years old! That didn't exactly inspire my confidence before surgery.

"This procedure took place in 1991, when laparoscopic surgery was just beginning to be used in this hospital. I was awakened at 5:00 a.m. to shower and prepare for surgery. I was first in line to be operated on and I was told that I would be back in my room by 9:30 a.m. All seemed to be going as scheduled. At 7:15 a.m., I was rolled into the operating room, and I was given an anesthetic at 7:30 a.m. What happened after that is a mystery. The doctor did explain to me a few weeks later that they had a late start that day.

"With laparoscopic surgery, four incisions are made in the abdomen, one being in the naval. Through one hole, they blow you up to look like you are nine months pregnant. Since I had just been pregnant, and all my muscles were stretched already, I probably blew up quite handily! I regained consciousness in the recovery room just before 2:00 p.m., sick from the anesthesia.

"The doctor never explained to me how much pain I would suffer after the surgery. Any comfort I gained was through comparing how I felt with the other woman who had been operated on that morning. We both experienced terrific pain in the chest area and shoulder blades as the gas strangely moved around in our chest cavities and dissipated. Pain medicine was requested, but it was denied to me because I was breastfeeding.

"That evening, my breasts were quite full and needed to be pumped. Since I was in so much pain, I requested that the breast pump be brought to my room. A handsome young orderly came jogging into my room. It was obvious he didn't have much experience operating a breast pump.

After a few unsuccessful tries, I exclaimed, 'Give me that thing!'

"The orderly happily complied: 'Ma'am, you probably know more about this machine than I do.'

"No kidding," I thought. With that, I turned the machine around, adjusted the wires, and got it going. Sometimes you have to look out for yourself while you're in the hospital. I felt pretty good about asserting myself and taking control of the situation, until I learned there was a lady in a semi-private room who had been in complete control. She had brought her own nurse with her!

"The next day, I became very impatient as I was ordered from one department to another. First, I went to the pulmonary clinic where a doctor requested to see the X-rays that showed the spot on my lung. Then, I went to the X-ray department where I found that the X-rays were unavailable in the records department. Next, I was referred for a CAT scan. The CAT scan revealed nothing on the lung, but it did reveal cysts on my liver. Finally, a sonogram revealed the cysts were insignificant.

"Three months after the birth, I was finally home free to enjoy my baby, who was almost too big to hold up in the air by then. I guess I experienced more complications than the average mom. Fibroids, gallstones, spots on the lungs, and cysts—some things my body can live with, some things just have to go. Through it all, and as time passes, the best possible outcome has been the joy of my son."

A Granddaughter's Baby

This was written by my third grandchild, who was 24 years old a year after her first baby's birth. Her husband had just finished medical school. I find her writing deliciously humorous!

"Not too long ago, I found myself six days shy of my due date. I was in such pain that any idea of actually waiting until the due date was wiped from the slate. As the midwife described, 'I was on the rollercoaster called labor.' She said, 'You can't get off in the middle, but like every rollercoaster, it has an end.' This was possibly the most encouraging thing about labor I'd heard so far—it has an end.

"During the first few hours, my husband and I were encouraged to stay home, relax, and make final preparations. I saw my husband set a new standard for his own ability to do housework. He loaded the car, changed the cat litter, did dishes, tidied up, and so on, and he was with me every five, four, or three minutes for a contraction.

"Oh, the plans I had made for just this time! When labor started, I was going to take a shower, do my hair, and put on a light amount of natural looking make-up. I'd even bought a trendy new sports bra to wear in the birthing pool. The ridiculous list of things I had planned rages on, but I will spare you. I had purchased every item I thought I might possibly need, but one thing I never thought of getting was new dishtowels. It hadn't even occurred to me. I found, though, that I enjoyed biting on a dishtowel when the contractions came, and wiping the sweat from my brow with it when they left. You couldn't have taken that towel from me for anything!

"We had taken several childbirth classes, and in each class the instructors stressed making sure that what we were experiencing was not false labor. Apparently, the hospital policy dictates that if you don't deliver your baby in two hours, you will be sent back home. What contradictory words—*false labor*. Nonetheless, I had trouble convincing myself that this was the real thing.

"Finally, when my contractions were two minutes apart, my husband insisted that we head for the hospital. With some coercion, I put on my shoes, and with my husband, my dishtowel, and 800 pounds of luggage, I headed for the hospital.

"At this point, I need to backtrack and explain my reasons for choosing to work with a midwife and for attempting a natural childbirth: I hate needles, and I hate the sight of blood. That pretty much sums up my reasoning. Blood, needles, IVs—these things tend to make me pass out. And for those who doubt my commitment to my admitted psychosomatic fear of needles, I offer my medication-free delivery as evidence.

"We arrived at the hospital around noon. As directed, we pulled into the valet parking area. Big mistake! No valets. Excruciating pain. Two more contractions. Ninety-five degree weather. Still no valet. My husband was running in circles, first around the car, then around the hospital. Still no valet. A few employees on their smoke break watched the scene from about 10 feet away. Then, a homeless man approached and said he would be happy to park the car.

"No valet, no valet, no valet! Finally, a gentleman brought over a wheelchair. That was about the time I decided to check out. Not able to bear the stares of spectators, I took my beloved dishtowel (*dishrag* may be a more appropriate term) and put it over my head. Oh, sweet peace! Now, I only had to worry about the pain.

"We eventually checked in, and were sent into the triage area of the emergency room. During this holding period, I peeked from under my cloth. After surveying the blistery rashes, blood, and gore around me, I decided to retreat again.

"I do remember an orderly passing my husband and me and offering to carry my luggage. 'Dang, lady! You got the doctor in there, too?' he exclaimed.

"Not too much later, we were wheeled to the elevator along with another pregnant woman and we began our ascension. My pain continued to intensify. This woman was not in active labor and did not look to be at full-term. When we left the elevator, we were both wheeled to the nurses' station where the nurse proceeded to tell us they only had one monitoring room left, and then asked which one of us wanted it. I am not prone to violence, but at that moment I would have *taken that woman out* to get that room. I'm talking a full-scale WWF Smackdown!

"They gave her the room.

"About 20 minutes later, we were given a room. The fetal monitors were in place and we were told that we needed to have 20 minutes of normal readings to enter the water-birthing room with the midwife. During that time, my husband stood glued to the computer screen. He told me he would let me know when contractions were coming. Like I didn't know!

"The nurse said that I was dilated to five centimeters and was fully effaced. We were quickly moved to the water-birthing room where I threw away my final ideas of how cute my birth was going to be. I grunted when my husband mentioned my sports bra, and I proceeded to make noises strikingly similar to a cow.

"Every few minutes, the phone would ring. 'What is the patient's last name?' I would spell it out and explain that I had indeed sent in my pre-admittance form. 'What is the patient's middle initial?'

"In the scope of things, how important is this information right now? The final blow came when my daughter's head was actually hanging out. They called and asked for my social security number!

"Birth is so amazing. As my husband was whispering a final prayer in my ear, our sweet Sophia was born. When we set eyes on her, we were so ready to go right back to the beginning, and do it all over again. It *is* like a roller coaster. No matter how scared you are—as soon as you get off the ride, all you want to do is run right back around and get in line again."

Food for Mothers

Here is a short note regarding the care of a new mother. It's an old fashioned idea, but most new mothers still appreciate meals delivered to their home after their baby is born, especially if there are other toddlers underfoot.

Here is a suggestion. Send bland food. Lasagnas, spaghetti, and pizza may be easy to prepare and transport, and the new mother might like that type of food. However, many have learned the hard way that babies do not. A newborn just can't handle all that spice, and will develop cramps and gas pains that are very painful, as told by that wincing smile they make. Do not send foods in the cabbage family, or any type of beans or lentils, which can also cause gas.

There are all kinds of good chicken casserole recipes that can be prepared. Also just fine are sweet potatoes, apple sauce, green bean casserole, scalloped potatoes, or roasted meats. Homemade soups and stews are delicious, too. Just go easy on the spices. If the baby could talk, he would say 'thank you.' Always remember that as long as the mother is breast feeding, the baby will be nourished by the same food served to the mother.

Hospital Rules

How to Protect Ourselves

During one of my hospital stays, a relative of a relative—who also happened to be a fellow patient—stepped into my room to make himself known and to visit. He was just inside the doorway when he gave a loose, robust cough. He'd been hospitalized for bronchitis and did not realize that I was very susceptible to it. I simply told him, as tactfully as possible, that I would love to visit with him at another time, when he was better. He understood and apologized for his unexpected cough.

Beware! Spreading germs like that from one room to the next in the hospital happens all the time.

I had a friend who liked to talk with her face about eight inches from mine. I tried backing away from her a number of times, but I did finally catch her bronchitis. I know that bronchitis is not the common cold, but cold germs can be spread the same way. In fact, cold germs can travel airborne for 10 to 15 feet.

Recently, I attended a funeral in a large, crowded church. I was seated toward the back, enjoying the music, when someone clear on the other side began coughing. I caught a glimpse of the woman as she coughed for the fourth time, but did not cover her mouth. I can tolerate a little coughing without being irritated, but this woman should have removed herself from the building and hacked it up. I know sometimes it's absolutely necessary to keep obligations, but she must have known how sick she was. She surely spread around a lot of germs that day.

Wearing a little face mask to keep from spreading germs is practiced in Japan. It makes a lot of sense. If we practiced just plain common sense and courtesy, we could eliminate a lot of sickness. Employers would love it, but the pharmaceutical companies would hate it. Have you ever noticed how many different cold medications there are in the drugstore?

Children are the worst offenders. Without giving any warning, they cough right in your face. Teachers, God bless them, must develop strong immune systems, or else they would all be dead.

One day, I picked up one of my precious grandchildren who gave me a kiss on the lips. Soon after, my daughter told me that she had just thrown up. Some kind of flu had made a run through the family, and this child had been the last one to get sick. Guess who was next? I never kiss anyone on the lips anymore. Instead, I give a gentle hug or just a slight brush on the cheek, unless of course, it's a kiss for my husband.

We are constantly exposed to colds, all winter long. In the hospital, we expect precautions to be taken by the nurses and staff. It's absolutely frightening to read the published lists in medical journals and newspapers of all of the deaths and injuries that occur in what we expect to be a safe haven—a hospital!

When a serious heart condition was discovered in a relative of mine, he was placed in a room in a local hospital before being transported to the University Hospital. I waited in the hall while a nurse prepared him. I heard her give a robust and contaminating cough before coming out into the hall.

I asked, "Did you cover your mouth when you coughed?"

She obviously did not like my question. It put her in a defensive mood. The nurse then motioned how she had put one hand over her mouth.

I asked, "Did you wash your hands?"

If looks could kill, I would have been in my grave from the way she glared at me, obviously wondering how I could dare to ask her or any nurse a question like that. It was clear that she had not washed her hands, and she quickly left to attend to another patient. I'll admit, it was quite bold of me. She knew I was serious.

Later, we were allowed to stand by the patient's bed. The nurse caring for the patient in Bed B gave the same kind of rugged cough, but covered her mouth with her hand. She quickly stepped to the sink to wash her hands. But just think, here was a patient on the way to having open heart surgery, being exposed to the common cold in the hospital! The common cold virus does not respond to any known antibiotic and must be fought off by the patient's own immune system. My relative, thankfully, escaped getting sick. His body had enough repairing to do after the invasive surgery.

My sister (the one with the heart problem described earlier) had a friend I will call Betty. I say "had," because Betty died. She was hospitalized for a problem with her heart, and she occupied Bed B. A person with a very bad cough was moved into her room to occupy Bed A. Betty stayed in that room with that coughing patient for three days until Betty was discharged. Two days later, she was admitted back into the hospital with a very bad cough. Her heart could not take the extra strain of all that coughing and Betty died in the hospital.

When my sister was hospitalized, and the person scheduled to occupy Bed B gave a productive cough on the way into her room, my sister grabbed her IV stand, bolted out of the room, and ordered the nurses to move her into another room. Remembering her friend Betty, she adamantly refused to go back into her assigned room with that sick patient. There were beds available in other rooms, some totally unoccupied, so a person with a communicable disease definitely didn't need to be placed in the same room as someone with a heart problem.

I don't think the admitting office is always well informed. That's when we, the patients, must take things into our own hands and make demands for our own safety. When there are other rooms available, it isn't necessary for you to stay with a very sick patient. If you want to get out of that hospital alive, speak up, or move yourself out. Ask yourself: "Do I want what this person has?" Don't let anyone tell you those coughs are not contagious.

The nurses probably won't like it if you decide on your own to move to a different room. It takes extra work to sterilize a bed, but then, you will be able to leave the hospital in a wheelchair instead of on a stretcher.

One very important thing that is sadly lacking in hospitals is fresh air. Schools, office buildings, and hospitals are all built with air-conditioning in mind. Closed air systems are probably cheaper and operate more efficiently. However, there is a time before summer and winter when the windows could be thrown open wide to let some of the germs out and to let a little healthy fresh air in.

A Good Night's Sleep

A restful night's sleep restores both the mind and the body. It is extremely essential for healing. Don't we go to hospitals to be healed? Then why don't they let us sleep?

There are doctors, lab technicians, TV repairmen, volunteers with reading material, kitchen help with meal trays, priests and ministers, visitors, and three shifts of nurses all to make sure that you are awake both day and night. And if your room is near the nurses' station where all the heavy record books are kept, the noise can sound like a factory.

Don't forget to consult with your doctor about omitting anything unnecessary during the night. In fact, if you ask, just about anything that you desire to make yourself more comfortable will usually be granted by your doctor, but only by your doctor. Tell him you don't want your vitals taken during the night, you would like a sleeping pill, you'd rather not have ice water at 2:00 a.m., and you don't need help to the bathroom at 3:00 a.m. He can put it in your records, and his requests will be followed by the hospital staff. The nurses have a relationship with the doctors and are bound to obey their orders. Patients, however, are another story.

Don't leave it to memory. Write your requests down if necessary, or have someone else do it for you if you are to be drugged, or are otherwise unable to do so. Don't be that patient whose needs get ignored.

Be sure to make your requests known the minute you see your doctor, because he comes and goes like the wind during his morning rounds, similar to the gingerbread man: Catch me, catch me, if you can. You can't catch me, I'm the doctor man!

One winter I was placed in a hospital room at the end of a corridor that seemed to capture all the heat in the building. I love to be warm, but it was just too hot for me to sleep there. After three days of complaining and several ignored requests to be moved, along with a visit from a plumber who rattled the pipes but accomplished nothing, it was still too hot. I packed my belongings, moved into an empty room down the hall that was comfortably cool, and had a good night's sleep. Nobody at the nurses' station liked it, but I was paying good money for that hospital room, and I believed I had the right to a room where the heat was working properly. A person feels bad enough after a surgery. Is it too much to ask for a comfortable night's sleep?

*

Recently, my sister suffered chest pains, and her husband, being the alarmist that he is, rushed her to the hospital at 2:00 in the morning. With her history of heart problems, she was placed in the Intensive Care Unit. She probably got to sleep around 3:30 in the morning. At 4:30 a.m., she was awakened from a sound sleep by a nurse who said, "I must bathe you now, so you'll be ready for breakfast."

She sleepily inquired, "What time is breakfast?"

"Eight o'clock," was the nurse's answer.

My sister is a bit on the timid side. If I were the patient, I would have said, "What in the world is the matter with you? I don't need three and a half hours to get ready for breakfast!"

She, being the *patient* patient that she is, allowed the nurse to bathe her. Then, at 5:30 a.m., the lab technician woke her to draw blood. When I visited her at 10:00 a.m., she looked exhausted. I helped her get comfortable so she could sleep. Her doctor had the privilege of waking her around 11:00 to give her the good news that he was discharging her.

That was one expensive breakfast.

I told her later that someone had once awakened me at 5:30 in the morning to fill my water pitcher. "Water!" she exclaimed, "I asked for a pitcher of ice water this morning, and just as I was leaving, the nurse came trudging into my room with my water pitcher. But when she realized that I was leaving, she took my pitcher away and I never did get a drink!"

During one hospital stay, a few hours after an afternoon surgery, I fell asleep only to be awakened by a nurse making a personal call on the Bed B phone. After listening to her idle chatter for five minutes, I asked her to leave. One thing you really *don't* want to do is make the nurses angry. Nurses can, if they want, make your hospital stay quite miserable. This nurse did nothing to retaliate because she knew that she was wrong to be using the phone in my room.

During another hospital stay, I rang the desk and politely asked for a sleeping tablet. I received an "okay" from the desk. Ten minutes later, I sweetly asked a second time and waited 15 minutes more. I am not one to use foul language. If by shouting the third request 30 minutes later hadn't worked, I think I would have used a few choice words to shock those nurses to attention. I finally got the pill.

It's true! Nurses will wake you up to give you a sleeping tablet. It actually happened to me on the last day of one of my hospital stays. I was to be discharged the next day, and was watching a good movie on TV. When the nurse with the medicine cart came at 10:00 p.m. to give me my sleeping pill, I requested, "May I please have that sleeping pill when the movie is over?"

I suppose there is a hospital rule that requires nurses to watch the patient swallow any medication, and this nurse would not bend the rule for me, even though she knew I was going home the next day. After all, it was only a sleeping tablet. But she would not trust me and give it to me, so I could take it myself later. I called the desk when the movie was over at about 11:00 p.m., and waited and waited for someone to bring that sleeping tablet. In the meantime, I fell asleep. At 1:00 a.m., I was rudely nudged by the same nurse with the pill in a dispensing cup. She seemed to have a gleam in her eye. I couldn't believe anyone would be so inconsiderate.

Then, of course, I couldn't go back to sleep. I decided that if I were ever in the same situation, I would take the pill, pretend to swallow it, spit it out, and take it later.

Better than that, now I just bring my own sleeping pills.

I am in favor of making an eleventh commandment: "Thou shalt not wake a sleeping patient to give him or her a sleeping pill."

Why should a patient have to go to so much trouble to be able get some sleep in a hospital?

*

There is an interesting mention of sleep in the first book in the Bible:

"The Lord God caused a deep sleep to fall upon Adam, and he slept, and he took one of his ribs, and closed up the flesh."

—Genesis 2:21

143

Now, whether or not we believe the creation story of Adam and Eve is inconsequential to the fact that the Bible says God performed the first surgery while Adam slept. It took man thousands of years to make the discovery that surgeries could be performed while a patient is under a deep sleep. So, if you can wake up from sleep in your own bed, in your own home, tomorrow morning, remember to give a word of thanks. You'll never appreciate sound, undisturbed sleep until you have been deprived of it by being in a hospital.

Pain Medication in the Hospital

The Hypo

Do you realize that rules in some hospitals state that *you* must ask for pain medication after surgery? Surgeons dole out pain medication very sparingly. Immediately after surgery, when things are pretty raw and healing has not begun, is when the pain medication is most appreciated and advantageous. I learned that the hard way when I suffered for two days after a hysterectomy until a visiting friend of mine asked, "Aren't they giving you anything for pain?"

"I don't know," I whined. "If they are, it sure isn't working." I was in so much pain, that I was barely coherent.

"Ring for the nurse. She will probably give you a hypo." This friend had first-hand knowledge of the pain I was enduring, because she'd had the same surgery a few months before.

I rang for the nurse. She gave me a shot, and in about a half an hour, I felt like a human being again. Doesn't it seem logical that a hospital staff should know how badly a patient feels six or seven hours after a hysterectomy?

The nurses never informed me about their policy on pain medication. At this hospital, patients were responsible for requesting medication if they felt they needed it. I was not coherent enough to ask. I am sure that if one of the male doctors had ever had a hysterectomy, plenty of pain killers would be ordered promptly, and they wouldn't be worried at all about becoming drug addicts. I'm not so sure they would allow themselves to be dragged out of bed the very next day, when the pain is just beginning to subside.

Here's the twelfth commandment I'd like to dictate to the doctors: "Thou shalt not drag all surgery patients to their feet the day after surgery.'

I know this practice of getting patients up onto their feet as quickly as possible began during or after World War II, and it seemed to work well with the young, physically fit soldiers who had been operated on for one reason or other. Many times, I suppose it was necessary to put them back on the battlefield. But come on now, have mercy! I'm sure some of us older ones could recover just as easily in bed.

My Only Experience with Morphine

I learned when I read my hospital bill that morphine had been used during the surgery I had, which was labeled a *posterior repair*. Don't ask. I wasn't in much pain afterwards due to the morphine, but my mind was extremely fuzzy for a whole day. I slightly recall my doctor's associate, who I had never met personally, standing at the end of my bed and checking my chart with the nurse. He probably took one look at my glassy eyes and didn't even bother to talk to me.

When I tried to sit up to eat, my head reeled in dizziness and I fell back down. My meal trays were carried away, barely touched, because I could not sit up to reach them. The morphine in my system had taken away my desire to eat—my normal hunger pains were not registering in my brain.

After two days, a petite nurse asked, "You haven't been up yet?"

"No one told me that I had to get up," was my reply.

"We must get you on your feet. Let me help you," she ordered. "You are going for a walk."

"I get so dizzy, I can't even sit up. I'm afraid I'll pass out," I answered.

"No, you won't," she assured me.

"Please, get someone to assist you," I insisted. "I am not about to jeopardize my recovery with an unnecessary fall."

I'm tall, and the nurse was very short. The effect of the morphine was beginning to wear off and it was good to be coming out of that gray area and to be able to think clearly again. I knew that if I fainted, though, it would be impossible for her to support me. I remembered a friend's unfortunate experience. She was allowed to fall, with three nurses standing nearby, and she struck her head after having brain surgery. It was fortunate that she did not die and become another statistic on the long list of accidental hospital fatalities.

My request for help did not seem unreasonable to me. The nurse, however, did not like my suggestion. She knew by the tone of my voice that I was not about to get up unless additional help was available. She left the room in a huff, probably muttering to herself, "Why do I get all the difficult patients?"

She returned shortly with a rather stout cleaning lady and the two of them attempted to assist me to my feet. I struggled to get to a sitting position, but I became so dizzy that I fell back down again. The two of them pulled me up again and dragged me to my feet. My head reeled and I immediately—with no warning—vomited on the floor. I felt badly, but not too badly, when some of it splattered on the nurse. I apologized.

She was absolutely right about standing up, though. Seconds after I did, I felt much better and all the dizziness left. I expected the nurse to be angry with me, but if she was, she didn't show it and she proceeded to mop the floor. I don't know if they were short of help in this hospital or not, but it seemed to me that it should have been a janitor's job to clean the floor.

The next morning, I was really hungry. I had eaten practically nothing for two days and I was looking forward with great anticipation to my breakfast. When I lifted the cover to the meal, it was clear that I'd been *under the influence* when I'd placed the order. There was no cream for my coffee, no milk for the cereal, and no butter or jam for the toast. I did not complain about my mistake, I just ate it anyway.

I left the hospital the third day after surgery, with a catheter, and I felt very thankful for the wheelchair ride. This was something new to me. Other times, the doctors had kept me in the hospital until the catheter had been removed.

Leaving the hospital alive, and without an infection, is always a happy day. Recovering at home in my own bed, I find, is much more comfortable and much more pleasant. Thank you, Medicare.

Be Good to Yourself

Stay Out of the Hospital

The hospital is a great place to avoid. The more frightening statistics I read, the more I realize how important it is to make my principal concern to get better as quickly as possible and to get out of the hospital alive.

Millions of patients have gone through the hospital system with no complications at all. It is, however, being discovered more and more that many have not. Neither you nor I want to become one of the *have nots*.

The *Journal of Healthcare Protection Management* reported that 20,254 crimes (yes, *crimes*) occurred in hospitals in one year. Add that to all the drug mix-ups that cause death, deaths caused by infections received while in the hospital, and fatalities resulting from just plain carelessness by an overworked staff, and hospitals can look like pretty scary places.

A good way to stay out of them is by being good to ourselves. These are the only bodies we will ever have, and if we want to enjoy life, we should take good care of them.

Learn to live, love, laugh, and let go. Here's a line from one of the ballads of the 1940s: *There will never ever be another you.*

Don't live in fear of hospitals. Just think! Millions come out alive and well, and it is the minority who are unfortunate. You don't stop taking a bath because 2,000 deaths a year occur as a result of a fall in a bathtub.

All these things that I had to learn the hard way have been shared with you so that you can profit by them. Perhaps they can help you to survive, and even enjoy, that hospital stay. Just remember, the doctors are gods, the nurses are angels, and you are that free spirit with a will and a mind of your own. It isn't mandatory for you to fit into their mold, because everyone is different.

Hospital policy differs from one hospital to the next. Doctors' treatments and opinions differ, and so do those of the nurses. If at all possible, take charge of your own treatment and ask questions about anything that you don't understand. It will help if you take these main precautions:

1. Never go to a hospital alone.

Take a good friend or a family member with you. Remember, if you are sick enough to go to a hospital, you're probably not in your best frame of mind. So, you need someone else there to help you make wise decisions and to serve as a second pair of ears to hear instructions. It is also a good idea to make a journal of all of your medicines and treatments. This information can then be shared with other caretakers. Doctors do not have the time to explain your condition to a number of caretakers.

2. Assume there are no stupid questions.

What are the names of the nurses?
Did you wash your hands?
What is the name of the medication?
What is the dosage?
What are the side effects?

What disease does my roommate have?

Is that equipment sterile?

What does the chart say about the surgery?

What medication will I be given for pain?

Must I ask for the pain medication after surgery?

This last question is very important. Make sure everyone is on the same page as far as the medications are concerned.

3. Review all X-rays and charts with your doctor.

Take time to read them! Ask to have everything on the X-rays pointed out to you. Study them. Your life may depend on it. I used to think that the record chart that is placed in the rack on the wall outside my room was some sort of hallowed material and that I wasn't allowed to read it. One time, I was tempted to take a peek, and I felt guilty for even thinking about it. I don't know why so much information is kept from the patient. Of course, if bad news is revealed in the file, some patients don't want to know. But if there is something we can do for ourselves, I believe the information should be shared.

4. Don't go to the emergency room on Sunday.

You will no doubt be put on hold until Monday, unless it truly is an emergency.

5. Keep your own records of your family's illnesses and treatments.

Many times, you will find your own answers within your own medical records.

6. Bring what you feel you need.

Ask your doctor if you can supplement the hospital diet with your own vitamins. Bring things from home that will aid in your comfort and well-being.

7. *Don't be afraid of appearing to be anti-social.*

Here's one I wish I'd thought of during my hospital stays, especially when I'd had surgery. Have the nurse hang a *Do Not Disturb* sign on your door until you feel well enough to enjoy company.

The Business of Medicine

Some patients will exhaust any or all treatments or cures available to regain their health, or to add another month, or even another day, to their lives on earth. The medical profession happily obliges, even though I believe in their hearts, the doctors know what will inevitably take place. The field of medicine is a business—a flourishing business.

We must remember that doctors are businessmen in white coats. Many have 10 to 12 years of study and hard work behind their degrees and they are not expected to work for a plumber's wages. They do a lot of good, and they deserve to be well paid. Many of us would not be alive were it not for the doctor's expertise.

But some of their fees are exorbitant. Hospital charges are even worse. One hospital charged me $5 for one sleeping tablet. The same brand of pills that I bought from the drug store were about 10 cents apiece. You would think that drugs would be cheaper in a hospital because they can obviously buy in volume.

Who really dictates how long we stay in the hospital? Is it the doctor? Or is it the insurance company? Or is it the government? I guess we are welcome to stay as long as the physicians keep ordering all those expensive, and sometimes needless, diagnostic tests. Another thing that always puzzled me is who owns the hospitals?

Recently, a young man I know was admitted to a hospital after suffering a brain aneurysm. His brother, a doctor affiliated with that hospital, stood by his bed, knowing that it was too late for any surgery. The man was in that bed for a total of 26 hours before he died. His widow received an invoice for $18,000 from the hospital.

When admitted to the hospital, you become a statistic in the record books. You are, for example, a married Caucasian female, age 27, in Room 232, Bed A or Bed B. Upon admittance, you give your life and medical history in exchange for one of those revealing gowns that make every part of your anatomy available for examination by the medical staff, as well as hospital hallway spectators. Next, you step on the scales (that in itself is depressing enough) and then you have your blood pressure and temperature taken. I always feel insulted when asked if I'm wearing dentures.

Then, even if you are fit enough to run a marathon, you are forced to accept a wheelchair ride to your room. That ride lets you know that you are no longer in control, and when the ID bracelet is snapped on, the deal is done. You are in the confines of the hospital until the good doctor releases you.

Since the government has become involved with different health-care programs, there seems to be a whole different mindset. It goes something like this: "I can do whatever I want; eat as much as I want, smoke or drink as much as I want; and I never have to think about the consequences of such abuse to my body because Big Brother will pay the bill."

Do people not understand that Medicare payments are drawn from the U.S. Treasury? We should never forget that the U.S. also stands for *Us*. We are the ones who put money into the U.S. Treasury.

My friend was in the hospital for two days and was charged almost $20,000. When she stood at the billing department desk to present her Medicare card, she questioned the charge by asking, "Do you think there could be a mistake?"

The answer enlightened her: "What do you care? You don't have to pay for it."

But we do pay for it in many ways. For instance, the price of a new car reflects the cost of health care provided for the employees of the manufacturer's company. The cost of supplemental insurance and private insurance is continually rising to accommodate the sometimes greedy and ridiculous charges we find on our statements.

I have, at times, insisted that the billing department itemize the charges on my hospital bill. When I find charges for services not rendered (for instance, a chest X-ray that was canceled), I confront them. Many times, I have been reimbursed. I find it only natural to check the charges on my home phone bill, on car repairs, or on any work I have contracted, so why shouldn't I have the privilege of looking over my hospital bill?

Beware, though. The itemized bill will not be given to you. It must be requested.

"The doctor of the future will give no medicine,
but will interest his patients in the care of the human frame,
in diet, and in the cause and prevention of disease."

—Thomas A. Edison

When Thomas Edison wrote his beliefs about medicine in the early 1900s, even in his wildest dreams, he would never have been able to imagine what our medical establishment has become today. He evidently knew how to take care of his health, because he lived to a ripe old age of 87 years.

Perhaps Thomas Edison's personal physician was keenly aware of the part of the Hippocratic Oath that states: I will apply dietetic measures for the benefit of the sick according to my ability and judgment. I will keep them from harm and injustice.

In my own experience, I have never been asked to discuss my diet with any doctor. Only once was I prescribed a dietary supplement of calcium by a chiropractor.

Edison did not foresee the rise of the multibillion-dollar pharmaceutical companies. Nor was he able to see all of the marvelous new scientific approaches to modern medicine that truly are remarkable.

Delicate open heart surgeries, organ transplants, dialysis, and many of the life-extending treatments practiced today were unheard of in his day.

None of the following health-destroying items were available for his use either: herbicides, pesticides, commercial fertilizers, food preservatives and additives, hydrogenated oils, food colorings, all those unpronounceable things printed on most packaged foods, altered seeds, homogenized milk, and refined flour that claims to have added vitamins, when, in truth, 13 nutrients are removed.

Doctors have not exactly followed Edison's advice. However, we can begin to take care of ourselves in our own way. There is no fountain of youth to be discovered, but good old common sense can sometimes work miracles.

Take Care of Yourself

When we fellow sufferers meet in various doctors' offices, therapy rooms, YMCAs, hospitals, or in the drug stores where we all get into a line that seems to be getting longer every year, we have opportunities to share our ailments.

Most patients appreciate someone who will simply listen to their problems of ill health. Some seek sympathy and others just plain want to talk about it. Oftentimes, by confiding with someone with a similar condition, it helps us to compare drugs, treatments, hospital confinements, how much time various doctors give to each patient, or the cost of various drugs that are prescribed.

I'm sure that doctors must get sick and tired of the whole lot of us streaming into their offices with our self-inflicted injuries and maladies. If we took better care of ourselves in the first place, and avoided their offices, we would all be better off.

"He's the best physician who knows the worthlessness
of most medicine."

—Benjamin Franklin

We don't exercise enough, we don't get enough sleep, we drink too much alcohol, we eat too much, and we don't drink enough water. I would think that some doctors would really like to scream at their patients, "Stop eating so much! You'll make yourself sick!" But they don't. They just wait for the inevitable to happen.

There are so many young men and women who are extremely overweight. While I was standing in line at the Burger King counter with my grandchildren, a young woman ahead of me ordered two large Whoppers, two large fries, and two large cokes. I watched as she squeezed into one of the booths, and I thought that perhaps a friend would be joining her. But no, she ate the whole order herself, as if she hadn't eaten for a week. If she keeps eating like that until she's 50 years old, when her metabolism changes, she's going to be in big trouble. Not only that, these large parents are allowing their children to overeat as well.

This was the headline of a Chicago newspaper article written by Lesley Tanner, an AP Medical writer:

IS OBESITY SURGERY AN OPTION FOR KIDS?

Drastic surgery for obesity, once viewed as suitable only for adults, is emerging as an option for children, a new pediatrics report says. Whether gastric bypass surgery, which shrinks the stomach from the size of a football to the size of an egg, might have long-term side effects for youngsters is unknown.

The article went on to report that approximately 10 pediatric surgeons had performed this surgery on children, all with positive results.

I have a good friend who opted for this type of surgery. For a while, it seemed to be successful. Her dress size of 24 dropped to a size 18. I bought a new dress for her to encourage her to keep up the good work, and she was so pleased with herself.

Three years later, she gained all that weight back. I believe she truly enjoys her overeating habits more than the satisfaction of having lost the weight. No surgery of this type can be considered a success unless the weight loss is permanent, and the only way to accomplish that goal is a drastic change in lifestyle. A lifelong, normal, healthy diet would eliminate the need for the surgery, and it would produce lasting results.

Knees are not made to take the punishment of supporting 300 or more pounds. Inevitably, the cartilage will wear too thin, and the pain and discomfort will cause these unsuspecting young people to seek the help of the *knee-ologists*. I have some lovely friends who have opted for knee replacements and surgeries. They were given no guarantees, and their surgeries have not always been successful.

There are two ways to learn, and this lesson should be observed and reinforced by family doctors with a warning to keep our weight under control. Food is so plentiful and cheap in this bountiful country. It takes common sense, and a look in a mirror, to let us know when we are eating too much. To me, living a totally sedentary life is terribly boring, but that's what many overeaters choose to do.

OVER THE LIPS
AND ONTO THE HIPS

Recently, I saw and heard the testimony of a 27-year-old woman on the Oprah Winfrey Show who had lost almost 300 pounds. She gave advice to the other obese women in the audience that I hope will inspire them to do the same.

She said, "You are hurting anyway. It only takes a year of a different kind of hurt to lose all the weight, and then you'll *have* a life."

Some of the women listening to her had beautiful facial features, and I could picture them being real knockouts if they would just follow through with the determination I saw in their faces. Some of them were facing death if they didn't lose weight. Of course, the underlying cause of their eating binges had to be dealt with first.

I read the following article in our local newspaper, written by an AP medical writer:

OBESITY LEADING TO
MORE HOSPITALIZATION FOR KIDS

Doctors have long warned that childhood obesity has become epidemic. But the new research is among the first to show how much more is at stake than fat children growing into fat adults—obesity can seriously sicken them now. The main concern is Type 2 diabetes, a dangerous disease that once struck mostly in middle age. Also, overweight children could become obese adults.

The Centers for Disease Control and Prevention reported that a disturbing increase in the numbers has made hospital costs related to childhood obesity more than triple in the past 20 years.

Supermarkets have aisle after aisle loaded with junk food. Instead of using snack foods as a treat, they are consumed as meals, and they are completely devoid of the nutrients necessary for good health.

A healthy way to shop in supermarkets is to stay on the perimeter where the fresh vegetables, meats and poultry, dairy, and whole grain breads can be found.

Nutrition should not be our doctor's problem. It's our responsibility to educate ourselves so that we don't become just another *patient* patient.

Afterword

"A word fitly spoken is like apples of gold in pictures of silver!"
—King Solomon, Proverbs 25:11

I don't know about you, but I don't like to be sick, or have painful things happen to me. I love life, and there is so much living to do. Basically, I am a very healthy, active person who just happened to experience all of those dumb things like heel spurs and nose warts. In this book, I wanted to share how I solved, or sometimes complicated, the problem, so that you could benefit from my mistakes and experiences and perhaps even find some humor in them.

Many times, I have considered that the purpose of my life is to bring joy into others' lives. Sure, I wake up some mornings feeling like I could chew nails. But then I remind myself that I live in a wonderful country, I have no debts, there is food in my refrigerator, I have wonderful friends and family, and I attend a good church that I can look forward to worshipping in every Sunday with no fear of oppression. Then I resume my grateful attitude. It is just as important to take care of your mind as it is to take care of your body.

I want to command the morning time. I want to open my eyes to the possibilities and opportunities before me. I want to take charge of my mind and focus on images of that which is true and beautiful. I want to reassure myself that each day has some purpose for me, even if it is hidden. It will be a great day when doctors can prescribe a pill for happiness. It could eliminate a number of diseases.

I heartily agree with Abraham Lincoln when he said, "A man can be just about as happy as he makes up his mind to be."

Printed in the United States
23926LVS00004B/151-300